Quick
Scripture
Reference
for
Counseling
Youth

D1316601

Quick Scripture Reference for Counseling Youth

PATRICIA A. MILLER
AND KEITH R. MILLER

BakerBooks
Grand Rapids, Michigan

Published by Baker Books
a division of Baker Publishing Group
P.O. Box 6287, Grand Rapids, MI 49516-6287
www.bakerbooks.com

Third printing, September 2008

Printed in the United States of America

Library of Congress Cataloging-in-Publication Data

Miller, Patricia A.
    Quick Scripture reference for counseling youth / Patricia A. Miller and Keith R. Miller.
       p. cm.
    ISBN 10: 0-8010-6608-5 (pbk. : alk. paper)
    ISBN 978: 0-8010-6608-5 (pbk. : alk. paper)
    1. Youth—Pastoral counseling of. 2. Church work with youth. 3. Youth—Religious life. I. Miller, Keith R. II. Title.
    BV4447.M498 2006
    259′.23—dc22
                                               2006001677

To
our parents,
Carl and Leona Miller
and Hank and Clara Voss.
You gave us a solid foundation in God's Word.
What a blessing you have been!

Subject Guide

Introduction

Purpose of This Book

This book was our hearts' desire many years ago, but being busy as a dad and mom, we were never able to put the time and energy into preparing it. Teenage years can be such a challenge. How we wish we could say we did everything right with our four children and were perfect examples of godly parents. What we discovered was that while logic, wisdom, and words were not always effective, the response to God's Word was dramatic. God couples with us through his Word to help guide the next generation.

In today's postmodern world, youth are aware of so much more of the issues of life and are constantly told there are no absolutes. More than ever, they need to have confidence in the things that will never change—God and his Word. As parents, youth leaders, and counselors, we often emphasize that God's Word is the answer for our needs. We are confident that our children and youth also must know it and its power. Why then are we so hesitant to use the Word? Is it because we are not familiar enough with Scripture ourselves to know where to find just the right text? It is our prayer that this book will assist greatly in that need. As we grow in our love of God and his Word, the result will be a relaxed and natural sharing of Scripture.

Many times we say to the college students with whom we work that if they are daily in God's Word, we do not fear for them. They may make mistakes, but they will not find themselves severely off target. They cannot be diligently in the Word and blatantly involved with sin. God's Word will keep them on the mark.

How to Use This Book

We have made every effort to be true to context. For those texts for which the context does not totally fit, we believe the principle (timeless, universal truth) does apply to the topic at hand.

Many of the Old Testament passages refer, in context, to Israel. Yet the principles reflecting God's care for his people and interest in their welfare can clearly be seen.

Our use of passages from the Mosaic law reflects our conviction that the traditional moral, civil, and ceremonial distinctions for that code are correct. God's moral law, as summarized in the Ten Commandments, is applicable for all people, for all time. Though the civil and ceremonial laws are not our rule of life in this age of grace, they do reflect the mind of God on issues of right and wrong. Thus we have drawn principles from them for the topics.

To avoid constant repetition of biblical texts, many of the topics provide cross-references to other related topics. Because of space limitations, some of the verses are not printed. Within each topic, references are listed for further study and application.

Suggestions for youth leaders and counselors:

- See our emphasis on the first topic, the plan of salvation.
- Have your Bible open as you counsel, as an excellent nonverbal emphasis on the value you place on God's Word.
- Ask all the youth to bring their own Bibles to the session. What God says to them is most important. Have them read, memorize, and underline.
- Cross-reference between topics to assist in finding the most applicable texts.
- Assign homework in the Word—something to study that week. Have the youth report back.
- Use the biblical illustrations at the end of many of the topics.
- Make sure the youth are having their quiet time!

Suggestions for parents:

- Use this book as a part of your family worship. Read and discuss topics and verses.

- Assign topics for study to your young people for areas in which they are struggling.
- Encourage them to memorize Scripture.
- Let your children see the importance of Scripture in your home. Let them see you having your quiet time, using the Word consistently.
- Let them know the Bible is the most important book in your home—and in the world!
- Keep thinking how you can naturally, and with ease, maintain a lifestyle consistently based on Scripture.

Suggestions for youth:

- Use the topics and verses for your quiet time.
- Memorize verses relevant to your needs.
- Seek wise counsel from more mature believers when you need it.
- Share the topics and verses with friends who are struggling.
- Prayerfully consider how you can help your friends with their problems.

Psalm 78:1–8

O my people, hear my teaching; listen to the words of my mouth. I will open my mouth in parables, I will utter hidden things, things from of old—what we have heard and known, what our fathers have told us. We will not hide them from their children; we will tell the next generation the praiseworthy deeds of the Lord, his power, and the wonders he has done. He decreed statutes for Jacob and established the law in Israel, which he commanded our forefathers to teach their children, so the next generation would know them, even the children yet to be born, and they in turn would tell their children. Then they would put their trust in God and would not forget his deeds but would keep his commands. They would not be like their forefathers—a stubborn and rebellious generation, whose hearts were not loyal to God, whose spirits were not faithful to him.

Plan of Salvation

This book is designed for believers who work with believers. Though much of Scripture is applicable and wise counsel and will help the nonbeliever, those with a personal relationship with God through Christ will have the greatest benefit.

Essential to any counseling situation is the need to ascertain if the young person has trusted in Jesus as the only way to heaven. If not, that is the counselor's first task. Only then will the Scripture, with the power of the Holy Spirit, be able to truly do its work.

Steps in guiding an individual to Christ (If possible, have counselees read the passages themselves from a Bible.)

1. **Each person is separated from God because of sin and sinful behavior.**

   Romans 3:23 For all have sinned and fall short of the glory of God.

   Isaiah 53:6 We all, like sheep, have gone astray, each of us has turned to his own way; and the LORD has laid on him the iniquity of us all.

2. **Sin must be punished—separation from God, hell.**

   Romans 6:23 For the wages of sin is death, but the gift of God is eternal life in Christ Jesus our Lord.

3. **There is nothing a person can do to gain status with God or to earn merit toward salvation.**

   Ephesians 2:8–9 For it is by grace you have been saved, through faith—and this not from yourselves, it is the gift of God—not by works, so that no one can boast.

Isaiah 64:6 All of us have become like one who is unclean, and all our righteous acts are like filthy rags; we all shrivel up like a leaf, and like the wind our sins sweep us away.

Titus 3:5

4. **Recognizing this dilemma, God had in place from creation a way for an individual to have a personal relationship with himself. The way was through the death of his Son, Jesus Christ.**

Romans 5:8 But God demonstrates his own love for us in this: While we were still sinners, Christ died for us.

John 3:16 For God so loved the world that he gave his one and only Son, that whoever believes in him shall not perish but have eternal life.

Acts 4:12 Salvation is found in no one else, for there is no other name under heaven given to men by which we must be saved.

Romans 10:9

5. **Each person must repent of his or her sin and personally believe (i.e., trust) in Jesus Christ as the only way to receive God's forgiveness and gain entrance into heaven.**

John 1:12 Yet to all who received him, to those who believed in his name, he gave the right to become children of God.

John 3:36 Whoever believes in the Son has eternal life, but whoever rejects the Son will not see life, for God's wrath remains on him.

Luke 15:7, 10; John 3:18; 14:6

6. **Salvation is assured.**

1 John 5:13 I write these things to you who believe in the name of the Son of God so that you may know that you have eternal life.

John 5:24 I tell you the truth, whoever hears my word and believes him who sent me has eternal life and will not be condemned; he has crossed over from death to life.

Biblical Model—John 3:14–18 with Numbers 21:6–9

Abortion

See also Unwed Pregnancy

Preventing an Abortion

1. **God is actively and personally involved in the life of every unborn person, even regarding plans for each day of his or her life.**

   Psalm 139:13–16 For you created my inmost being; you knit me together in my mother's womb. I praise you because I am fearfully and wonderfully made; your works are wonderful, I know that full well. My frame was not hidden from you when I was made in the secret place. When I was woven together in the depths of the earth, your eyes saw my unformed body. All the days ordained for me were written in your book before one of them came to be.

2. **The prophets recognized that God knew them as persons before they were born.**

   Jeremiah 1:5 Before I formed you in the womb I knew you, before you were born I set you apart; I appointed you as a prophet to the nations.

   Isaiah 49:1 Listen to me, you islands; hear this, you distant nations: Before I was born the LORD called me; from my birth he has made mention of my name.

3. **Elizabeth's unborn baby was aware of the unborn child Mary carried. Though a unique situation (the God-man in the womb), evidence is provided for personhood in the womb.**

   Luke 1:44 As soon as the sound of your greeting reached my ears, the baby in my womb leaped for joy.

4. **Children are a reward—a gift—from God, no matter how their conception began.**

   Psalm 127:3–4 Sons are a heritage from the LORD, children a reward from him. Like arrows in the hands of a warrior are sons born in one's youth.

5. **Following what self wants, rather than what God wants, is sin and leads to problems.**

   Proverbs 14:12 There is a way that seems right to a man, but in the end it leads to death.

   Proverbs 16:2 All a man's ways seem innocent to him, but motives are weighed by the LORD.

   Philippians 2:3–4 Do nothing out of selfish ambition or vain conceit, but in humility consider others better than yourselves. Each of you should look not only to your own interests, but also to the interests of others.

   Romans 8:5–6; 2 Timothy 3:1–2

6. **Our actions are not hidden from God.**

   Hebrews 4:13 Nothing in all creation is hidden from God's sight. Everything is uncovered and laid bare before the eyes of him to whom we must give account.

7. **Our bodies are not ours—they belong to God.**

   1 Corinthians 6:19 Do you not know that your body is a temple of the Holy Spirit, who is in you, whom you have received from God? You are not your own.

   Romans 12:1–2; 2 Corinthians 6:16

After an Abortion (See also Confession, Forgiveness, Past Memories)

1. **When forgiveness is requested, it is granted without reservation.**

   Psalm 32:3–5 When I kept silent, my bones wasted away through my groaning all day long. For day and night your hand was heavy upon me; my strength was sapped as in the heat of summer. Then I acknowledged my sin to you and did not cover up my iniquity. I said,

"I will confess my transgressions to the Lord"—and you forgave the guilt of my sin.

2. God can take our broken spirits and produce joy.

Psalm 51:12–17 Restore to me the joy of your salvation and grant me a willing spirit, to sustain me. Then I will teach transgressors your ways, and sinners will turn back to you. Save me from bloodguilt, O God, the God who saves me, and my tongue will sing of your righteousness. O Lord, open my lips, and my mouth will declare your praise. You do not delight in sacrifice, or I would bring it; you do not take pleasure in burnt offerings. The sacrifices of God are a broken spirit; a broken and contrite heart, O God, you will not despise.

3. God offers restoration.

Psalm 40:1–3 I waited patiently for the Lord; he turned to me and heard my cry. He lifted me out of the slimy pit, out of the mud and mire; he set my feet on a rock and gave me a firm place to stand. He put a new song in my mouth, a hymn of praise to our God. Many will see and fear and put their trust in the Lord.

4. God understands the women of Israel weeping for children they would never see again. He understands sorrow for the loss of children.

Jeremiah 31:15 This is what the Lord says: "A voice is heard in Ramah, mourning and great weeping, Rachel weeping for her children and refusing to be comforted, because her children are no more."

5. As those in Israel's captivity were not to dwell on the awfulness of the captivity, so we also are not to dwell on the past once it is forgiven.

Isaiah 43:18–19 Forget the former things; do not dwell on the past. See, I am doing a new thing! Now it springs up; do you not perceive it? I am making a way in the desert and streams in the wasteland.

6. God is the only one who can comfort us in our sorrow.

Psalm 18:1–6 I love you, O Lord, my strength. The Lord is my rock, my fortress and my deliverer; my God is my rock, in whom I take refuge. He is my shield and the horn of my salvation, my stronghold. I call to the LORD, who is worthy of praise, and I am saved from my enemies. The cords of death entangled me; the torrents of destruction overwhelmed me. The cords of the grave coiled around me; the snares of death confronted me. In my distress I called to the LORD; I cried to my God for help. From his temple he heard my voice; my cry came before him, into his ears.

Isaiah 25:8

Biblical Illustration—Mary and Elizabeth (Luke 1:26–45)

Abuse

See also Suffering, Past Memories, Rape, Incest

1. Others may fail us, but God always stands by us.

Psalm 37:39–40 The salvation of the righteous comes from the Lord; he is their stronghold in time of trouble. The Lord helps them and delivers them; he delivers them from the wicked and saves them, because they take refuge in him.

Psalm 72:12 For he will deliver the needy who cry out, the afflicted who have no one to help.

Lamentations 3:20–23 I well remember them, and my soul is downcast within me. Yet this I call to mind and therefore I have hope: Because of the Lord's great love we are not consumed, for his compassions never fail. They are new every morning; great is your faithfulness.

Joshua 1:9; Isaiah 25:4

2. God is always present, even when we feel alone.

Psalm 139:7–10 Where can I go from your Spirit? Where can I flee from your presence? If I go up to the heavens, you are there; if I make my bed in the depths, you are there. If I rise on the wings of the dawn, if I settle on the far side of the sea, even there your hand will guide me, your right hand will hold me fast.

Psalm 46:1 God is our refuge and strength, an ever-present help in trouble.

Psalm 142:3–6 When my spirit grows faint within me, it is you who know my way. In the path where I walk men have hidden a snare for me. Look to my right and see; no one is concerned for me. I have no refuge; no one cares for my life. I cry to you, O LORD; I say, "You are my refuge, my portion in the land of the living." Listen to my cry, for I am in desperate need; rescue me from those who pursue me, for they are too strong for me.

Lamentations 3:57–60

3. David prayed for safety from evil men. We can do the same.

Psalm 69:13–18 But I pray to you, O LORD, in the time of your favor; in your great love, O God, answer me with your sure salvation. Rescue me from the mire, do not let me sink; deliver me from those who hate me, from the deep waters. Do not let the floodwaters engulf me or the depths swallow me up or the pit close its mouth over me. Answer me, O LORD, out of the goodness of your love; in your great mercy turn to me. Do not hide your face from your servant; answer me quickly, for I am in trouble. Come near and rescue me; redeem me because of my foes.

Psalm 140:1–5

4. We must not allow past events to control the present life. When there is nothing we can do to correct the past, we must commit it to God's future care.

Isaiah 43:18–19 Forget the former things; do not dwell on the past. See, I am doing a new thing! Now it springs up; do you not perceive it? I am making a way in the desert and streams in the wasteland.

Matthew 11:28–30 Come to me, all you who are weary and burdened, and I will give you rest. Take my yoke upon you and learn from me, for I am gentle and humble in heart, and you will find rest for your souls. For my yoke is easy and my burden is light.

Philippians 3:13–14

Biblical Illustrations—Jesus, trial and crucifixion; Hagar (Genesis 16); David abused by Saul (1 Samuel 18–26)

Note: It is good that the abused person is seeking your counsel, but others (parents, doctors, school, government) must get involved as well for relief to occur. Counselors must report abuse as required by law.

Adoption

See also Orphan

1. **God has a special interest in individuals who for some reason are left without biological parents.**

    Psalm 27:10 Though my father and mother forsake me, the LORD will receive me.

    Isaiah 49:15 Can a mother forget the baby at her breast and have no compassion on the child she has borne? Though she may forget, I will not forget you!

    Ezekiel 34:11–16

2. **Whether an individual is with a biological family or an adopted family, God is intimately involved in his or her life.**

    Psalm 139:16 Your eyes saw my unformed body. All the days ordained for me were written in your book before one of them came to be.

    Psalm 10:14 But you, O God, do see trouble and grief; you consider it to take it in hand. The victim commits himself to you; you are the helper of the fatherless.

    Deuteronomy 10:18 He defends the cause of the fatherless and the widow, and loves the alien, giving him food and clothing.

    Jeremiah 29:11

3. **God adopts us into his family at the point of our salvation.**

    Ephesians 1:5 He predestined us to be adopted as his sons through Jesus Christ, in accordance with his pleasure and will.

23

Romans 8:23 Not only so, but we ourselves, who have the firstfruits of the Spirit, groan inwardly as we wait eagerly for our adoption as sons, the redemption of our bodies.

Galatians 4:7

4. God looks favorably on those who care for orphans.

James 1:27 Religion that God our Father accepts as pure and faultless is this: to look after orphans and widows in their distress and to keep oneself from being polluted by the world.

Matthew 25:40

Biblical Illustration—Esther 2:15; 4:14

Anger

See also Bitterness, Forgiving Others

1. **Both the Father and the Son expressed righteous anger against sin. This is the only acceptable anger a believer should express.**

    Romans 1:18 The wrath of God is being revealed from heaven against all the godlessness and wickedness of men who suppress the truth by their wickedness.

    Mark 3:5 He looked around at them in anger and, deeply distressed at their stubborn hearts, said to the man, "Stretch out your hand." He stretched it out, and his hand was completely restored.

    Exodus 32:10

2. **Sinful anger is included in a list of equally disturbing sins.**

    Galatians 5:19–21 The acts of the sinful nature are obvious: sexual immorality, impurity and debauchery; idolatry and witchcraft; hatred, discord, jealousy, fits of rage, selfish ambition, dissensions, factions and envy; drunkenness, orgies, and the like. I warn you, as I did before, that those who live like this will not inherit the kingdom of God.

    Proverbs 29:22 An angry man stirs up dissension, and a hot-tempered one commits many sins.

3. **Anger is loss of control and must be removed.**

    Proverbs 29:11 A fool gives full vent to his anger, but a wise man keeps himself under control.

    Ephesians 4:31–32 Get rid of all bitterness, rage and anger, brawling and slander, along with every form of malice. Be kind and compassionate to one another, forgiving each other, just as in Christ God forgave you.

Psalm 37:8; Colossians 3:8

4. **Avoiding anger requires listening, talking less, proceeding slowly, and not reacting.**

Proverbs 20:3 It is to a man's honor to avoid strife, but every fool is quick to quarrel.

Ecclesiastes 7:9 Do not be quickly provoked in your spirit, for anger resides in the lap of fools.

James 1:19–20 My dear brothers, take note of this: Everyone should be quick to listen, slow to speak and slow to become angry, for man's anger does not bring about the righteous life that God desires.

Proverbs 14:17

5. **The practice of answering gently, and not with returned anger, will help reduce the occurrence of anger.**

Proverbs 15:1 A gentle answer turns away wrath, but a harsh word stirs up anger.

Proverbs 15:18 A hot-tempered man stirs up dissension, but a patient man calms a quarrel.

Proverbs 20:22

6. **If anger occurs, the issue should be resolved that day or, at the very least, a specific plan made that day for resolution.**

Ephesians 4:26 "In your anger do not sin": Do not let the sun go down while you are still angry.

Psalm 4:4 In your anger do not sin; when you are on your beds, search your hearts and be silent.

7. **Practice patience, the contrast to anger.**

Proverbs 14:29 A patient man has great understanding, but a quick-tempered man displays folly.

Proverbs 15:18 A hot-tempered man stirs up dissension, but a patient man calms a quarrel.

Proverbs 16:32

8. **People who have a tendency toward anger are not the best choices for friends (or marriage partners).**

Proverbs 22:24–25 Do not make friends with a hot-tempered man, do not associate with one easily angered, or you may learn his ways and get yourself ensnared.

Proverbs 21:19 Better to live in a desert than with a quarrelsome and ill-tempered wife.

Psalm 119:63; Proverbs 19:19

Attitude/Mind

See also Thought Life

1. **Loving God must have first priority in our thinking.**

    Matthew 22:37 Jesus replied: "Love the Lord your God with all your heart and with all your soul and with all your mind."

    Deuteronomy 10:12 And now, O Israel, what does the LORD your God ask of you but to fear the LORD your God, to walk in all his ways, to love him, to serve the LORD your God with all your heart and with all your soul.

    Joshua 23:11

2. **We must maintain an eternal perspective in our thinking.**

    Colossians 3:2 Set your minds on things above, not on earthly things.

    2 Corinthians 4:18 So we fix our eyes not on what is seen, but on what is unseen. For what is seen is temporary, but what is unseen is eternal.

    Romans 14:7–8

3. **Our minds must be focused on spiritual things, i.e., what God desires for us.**

    Romans 8:5–8 Those who live according to the sinful nature have their minds set on what that nature desires; but those who live in accordance with the Spirit have their minds set on what the Spirit desires. The mind of sinful man is death, but the mind controlled by the Spirit is life and peace; the sinful mind is hostile to God. It does not submit to God's law, nor can it do so. Those controlled by the sinful nature cannot please God.

4. We must have transformed, renewed minds and must not think as unbelievers think.

Romans 12:2 Do not conform any longer to the pattern of this world, but be transformed by the renewing of your mind. Then you will be able to test and approve what God's will is—his good, pleasing and perfect will.

Ephesians 4:17–18, 22–24 So I tell you this, and insist on it in the Lord, that you must no longer live as the Gentiles do, in the futility of their thinking. They are darkened in their understanding and separated from the life of God because of the ignorance that is in them due to the hardening of their hearts. . . . You were taught, with regard to your former way of life, to put off your old self, which is being corrupted by its deceitful desires; to be made new in the attitude of your minds; and to put on the new self, created to be like God in true righteousness and holiness.

5. Firm decisions are necessary for areas of conduct not specifically dealt with in Scripture.

Romans 14:5 One man considers one day more sacred than another; another man considers every day alike. Each one should be fully convinced in his own mind. [See context.]

6. We must think sacrificially, placing others ahead of ourselves.

John 15:13 Greater love has no one than this, that he lay down his life for his friends.

Philippians 2:3, 5–7 Do nothing out of selfish ambition or vain conceit, but in humility consider others better than yourselves. . . . Your attitude should be the same as that of Christ Jesus: Who, being in very nature God, did not consider equality with God something to be grasped, but made himself nothing, taking the very nature of a servant, being made in human likeness.

Ephesians 4:2

7. **We must develop a proper view of ourselves, being humble, not prideful.**

Romans 12:3 For by the grace given me I say to every one of you: Do not think of yourself more highly than you ought, but rather think of yourself with sober judgment, in accordance with the measure of faith God has given you.

Romans 12:16 Live in harmony with one another. Do not be proud, but be willing to associate with people of low position. Do not be conceited.

Proverbs 16:18; 18:12

8. **Prayer and correct thinking produce minds that overcome worry.**

Philippians 4:6–8 Do not be anxious about anything, but in everything, by prayer and petition, with thanksgiving, present your requests to God. And the peace of God, which transcends all understanding, will guard your hearts and your minds in Christ Jesus. Finally, brothers, whatever is true, whatever is noble, whatever is right, whatever is pure, whatever is lovely, whatever is admirable—if anything is excellent or praiseworthy—think about such things.

Authority/Rebellion/Submission

See also Work Ethic

1. Each individual must acknowledge God as the ultimate authority.

Jeremiah 7:23 But I gave them this command: Obey me, and I will be your God and you will be my people. Walk in all the ways I command you, that it may go well with you.

Psalm 25:7 Remember not the sins of my youth and my rebellious ways; according to your love remember me, for you are good, O LORD.

Ecclesiastes 12:13 Now all has been heard; here is the conclusion of the matter: Fear God and keep his commandments, for this is the whole duty of man.

Psalm 119:59–60; John 15:10–11; 1 Peter 1:14–15

2. Rebellious attitudes and actions are sinful and will bring God's discipline.

Isaiah 63:10 Yet they rebelled and grieved his Holy Spirit. So he turned and became their enemy and he himself fought against them.

Isaiah 65:2 All day long I have held out my hands to an obstinate people, who walk in ways not good, pursuing their own imaginations.

1 Samuel 15:23; Isaiah 1:19–20

3. God commands young people to be in submission to their parents.

Colossians 3:20 Children, obey your parents in everything, for this pleases the Lord.

Proverbs 6:20 My son, keep your father's commands and do not forsake your mother's teaching.

Proverbs 23:22–25 Listen to your father, who gave you life, and do not despise your mother when she is old. Buy the truth and do not sell it; get wisdom, discipline and understanding. The father of a righteous man has great joy; he who has a wise son delights in him. May your father and mother be glad; may she who gave you birth rejoice!

Proverbs 12:1; 13:1; Ephesians 6:2–3; 2 Timothy 3:2

4. God has established governmental authorities for our good.

Romans 13:1, 4–5 Everyone must submit himself to the governing authorities, for there is no authority except that which God has established. The authorities that exist have been established by God. ... For he is God's servant to do you good. But if you do wrong, be afraid, for he does not bear the sword for nothing. He is God's servant, an agent of wrath to bring punishment on the wrongdoer. Therefore, it is necessary to submit to the authorities, not only because of possible punishment but also because of conscience.

1 Peter 2:13–15

5. Respect must be given to other adults, including school authorities.

1 Peter 5:5 Young men, in the same way be submissive to those who are older. All of you, clothe yourselves with humility toward one another, because, "God opposes the proud but gives grace to the humble."

Titus 3:1–2 Remind the people to be subject to rulers and authorities, to be obedient, to be ready to do whatever is good, to slander no one, to be peaceable and considerate, and to show true humility toward all men.

1 Peter 2:17

6. Church leaders are to be respected and obeyed.

Hebrews 13:17 Obey your leaders and submit to their authority. They keep watch over you as men who must give an account. Obey them so that their work will be a joy, not a burden, for that would be of no advantage to you.

1 Thessalonians 5:12–13; Hebrews 13:7

Biblical Illustrations—Tower of Babel (Genesis 11); Esau (Genesis 28:6–9); sons of Eli (1 Samuel 2:22–25); Saul (1 Samuel 15); Jesus (Luke 2:51–52); prodigal son (Luke 15:11–32)

Bitterness

See also Forgiving Others, Attitude

1. **Bitterness is sin and adversely affects others and ourselves.**

   Hebrews 12:15 See to it that no one misses the grace of God and that no bitter root grows up to cause trouble and defile many.

   James 3:14–16 But if you harbor bitter envy and selfish ambition in your hearts, do not boast about it or deny the truth. Such "wisdom" does not come down from heaven but is earthly, unspiritual, of the devil. For where you have envy and selfish ambition, there you find disorder and every evil practice.

2. **Bitterness, as a mark of the unsaved, is an unacceptable emotion for a believer.**

   Romans 3:14 Their mouths are full of cursing and bitterness.

   Acts 8:23 For I see that you are full of bitterness and captive to sin.

3. **Bitterness needs to be removed through kindness, compassion, and forgiveness.**

   Ephesians 4:31–32 Get rid of all bitterness, rage and anger, brawling and slander, along with every form of malice. Be kind and compassionate to one another, forgiving each other, just as in Christ God forgave you.

4. **Each person has his or her own areas of bitterness to work on.**

   Proverbs 14:10 Each heart knows its own bitterness, and no one else can share its joy.

5. **God is sovereign over everything that has happened, so trust his perfect plan.**

   Romans 8:28 And we know that in all things God works for the good of those who love him, who have been called according to his purpose.

   Romans 12:17–19 Do not repay anyone evil for evil. Be careful to do what is right in the eyes of everybody. If it is possible, as far as it depends on you, live at peace with everyone. Do not take revenge, my friends, but leave room for God's wrath, for it is written: "It is mine to avenge; I will repay," says the Lord.

   Psalm 37:1–2

Biblical Illustrations—Esau with Jacob (Genesis 32–33); David (Psalm 37)

Broken Heart

See also Suffering, Depression, Death

1. God knows and cares about our broken hearts.

Psalm 56:8 Record my lament; list my tears on your scroll—are they not in your record?

Isaiah 61:1 The Spirit of the Sovereign LORD is on me, because the LORD has anointed me to preach good news to the poor. He has sent me to bind up the brokenhearted, to proclaim freedom for the captives and release from darkness for the prisoners.

Isaiah 57:15 For this is what the high and lofty One says—he who lives forever, whose name is holy: "I live in a high and holy place, but also with him who is contrite and lowly in spirit, to revive the spirit of the lowly and to revive the heart of the contrite."

John 11:33–36

2. God is in charge of the events of our lives. He knows what is best.

Proverbs 19:21 Many are the plans in a man's heart, but it is the LORD's purpose that prevails.

Isaiah 25:1 O LORD, you are my God; I will exalt you and praise your name, for in perfect faithfulness you have done marvelous things, things planned long ago.

Jeremiah 29:11–13 "For I know the plans I have for you," declares the LORD, "plans to prosper you and not to harm you, plans to give you hope and a future. Then you will call upon me and come and pray to me, and I will listen to you. You will seek me and find me when you seek me with all your heart."

Psalm 33:11; Romans 8:28

3. God will respond to our needs. Relief is coming.

Psalm 34:18 The LORD is close to the brokenhearted and saves those who are crushed in spirit.

Psalm 147:3 He heals the brokenhearted and binds up their wounds.

Ecclesiastes 3:11 He has made everything beautiful in its time. He has also set eternity in the hearts of men; yet they cannot fathom what God has done from beginning to end.

John 14:1, 27 Do not let your hearts be troubled. Trust in God; trust also in me. . . . Peace I leave with you; my peace I give you. I do not give to you as the world gives. Do not let your hearts be troubled and do not be afraid.

Psalm 42:5–6; 116:7–9

4. When we are hurting, God can use that hurt and the comfort he gives us to help others who are hurting.

2 Corinthians 1:3–4 Praise be to the God and Father of our Lord Jesus Christ, the Father of compassion and the God of all comfort, who comforts us in all our troubles, so that we can comfort those in any trouble with the comfort we ourselves have received from God.

Career

See Choices, Future Plans, Work Ethic

1. **Parents should encourage their children toward individual choices and interests in career decisions.**

    Proverbs 22:6 Train a child in the way he should go, and when he is old he will not turn from it.

    ["In the way he should go" is literally "according to his natural bent."]

2. **Forcing a career decision on a child could be a violation of the command for parents (especially fathers) to not exasperate their children.**

    Ephesians 6:4 Fathers, do not exasperate your children; instead, bring them up in the training and instruction of the Lord.

    Colossians 3:21 Fathers, do not embitter your children, or they will become discouraged.

3. **Seeking God's wisdom in any matter, including career choices, is always essential.**

    James 1:5 If any of you lacks wisdom, he should ask God, who gives generously to all without finding fault, and it will be given to him.

4. **As we trust in God completely, allowing him to give us direction for the pathways of our lives, we can be confident that his leading is sure.**

    Proverbs 3:5–6 Trust in the LORD with all your heart and lean not on your own understanding; in all your ways acknowledge him, and he will make your paths straight.

Psalm 20:4–5 May he give you the desire of your heart and make all your plans succeed. We will shout for joy when you are victorious and will lift up our banners in the name of our God. May the LORD grant all your requests.

Joshua 1:9; Proverbs 4:25–26

5. **Whatever career choice is made, all work must be done ultimately for God's glory.**

Colossians 3:17 And whatever you do, whether in word or deed, do it all in the name of the Lord Jesus, giving thanks to God the Father through him.

Colossians 3:23 Whatever you do, work at it with all your heart, as working for the Lord, not for men.

1 Corinthians 10:31; 2 Thessalonians 1:11–12

6. **A young man who chooses to be a husband and father must make that calling his first and foremost career responsibility.**

Ephesians 5:25, 28 Husbands, love your wives, just as Christ loved the church and gave himself up for her. . . . In this same way, husbands ought to love their wives as their own bodies. He who loves his wife loves himself.

Deuteronomy 6:6–7 These commandments that I give you today are to be upon your hearts. Impress them on your children. Talk about them when you sit at home and when you walk along the road, when you lie down and when you get up.

Psalm 128:1–4; Matthew 7:9–11

7. **A young woman who chooses to be a wife and mother must make that calling her first and foremost career responsibility.**

Titus 2:3–5 Likewise, teach the older women to be reverent in the way they live, not to be slanderers or addicted to much wine, but to teach what is good. Then they can train the younger women to love their husbands and children, to be self-controlled and pure, to be busy at home, to be kind, and to be subject to their husbands, so that no one will malign the word of God.

8. **While every Christian is called to total service for God, his or her call to vocational Christian service (if it is given) must also be accepted.**

Matthew 9:37–38 Then he said to his disciples, "The harvest is plentiful but the workers are few. Ask the Lord of the harvest, therefore, to send out workers into his harvest field."

Isaiah 6:8 Then I heard the voice of the Lord saying, "Whom shall I send? And who will go for us?" And I said, "Here am I. Send me!"

Isaiah 52:7; John 4:35

Biblical Illustrations—Joseph narratives (Genesis 39–45); prophets—Elisha, Jeremiah, Isaiah, Amos; disciples—Simon, Andrew, James, John (Mark 1:16–20)

Choices/Decision Making/God's Will

See also Career, Future Plans, Peer Pressure

1. **Prayer for wisdom in every decision is essential.**

    James 1:5 If any of you lacks wisdom, he should ask God, who gives generously to all without finding fault, and it will be given to him.

    Psalm 25:4–5 Show me your ways, O LORD, teach me your paths; guide me in your truth and teach me, for you are God my Savior, and my hope is in you all day long.

    Jeremiah 10:23 I know, O LORD, that a man's life is not his own; it is not for man to direct his steps.

    James 3:17

2. **Knowing God's will requires a submissive heart.**

    Psalm 40:8 I desire to do your will, O my God; your law is within my heart.

    Jeremiah 6:16 This is what the LORD says: "Stand at the crossroads and look; ask for the ancient paths, ask where the good way is, and walk in it, and you will find rest for your souls. But you said, 'We will not walk in it.'"

    Hosea 14:9; Romans 12:1–2; James 4:13–15

3. **When we proceed with a yielded heart, God will provide direction, even when we must choose between two equally good decisions.**

    Psalm 25:12–14 Who, then, is the man that fears the LORD? He will instruct him in the way chosen for him. He will spend his days in prosperity, and his descendants will inherit the land. The LORD confides in those who fear him; he makes his covenant known to them.

Proverbs 4:11–13 I guide you in the way of wisdom and lead you along straight paths. When you walk, your steps will not be hampered; when you run, you will not stumble. Hold on to instruction, do not let it go; guard it well, for it is your life.

Psalm 48:14 For this God is our God for ever and ever; he will be our guide even to the end.

Proverbs 3:5–6; Isaiah 42:16

4. **God is sovereign and has a plan in which we can have complete confidence.**

Isaiah 25:1 O LORD, you are my God; I will exalt you and praise your name, for in perfect faithfulness you have done marvelous things, things planned long ago.

Psalm 138:8 The LORD will fulfill his purpose for me; your love, O LORD, endures forever—do not abandon the works of your hands.

Psalm 37:23–24; Jeremiah 29:11–13

5. **Never make a decision contrary to the Word of God.**

Deuteronomy 5:29 Oh, that their hearts would be inclined to fear me and keep all my commands always, so that it might go well with them and their children forever!

Proverbs 4:25–27 Let your eyes look straight ahead, fix your gaze directly before you. Make level paths for your feet and take only ways that are firm. Do not swerve to the right or the left; keep your foot from evil.

2 Timothy 3:16–17 All Scripture is God-breathed and is useful for teaching, rebuking, correcting and training in righteousness, so that the man of God may be thoroughly equipped for every good work.

Isaiah 30:1; 55:8

6. **Determining God's will involves seeking the counsel of strong Christians who are wise.**

   Proverbs 11:14 For lack of guidance a nation falls, but many advisers make victory sure.

   Proverbs 15:22 Plans fail for lack of counsel, but with many advisers they succeed.

7. **What God desires for our lives is found in his Word.**

   Deuteronomy 32:46–47 Take to heart all the words I have solemnly declared to you this day, so that you may command your children to obey carefully all the words of this law. They are not just idle words for you—they are your life.

   Joshua 1:8 Do not let this Book of the Law depart from your mouth; meditate on it day and night, so that you may be careful to do everything written in it. Then you will be prosperous and successful.

   Psalm 119:105; Micah 6:8

8. **Determining God's will involves prayer for ourselves as well as others praying for us.**

   Colossians 1:9–11 For this reason, since the day we heard about you, we have not stopped praying for you and asking God to fill you with the knowledge of his will through all spiritual wisdom and understanding. And we pray this in order that you may live a life worthy of the Lord and may please him in every way: bearing fruit in every good work, growing in the knowledge of God, being strengthened with all power according to his glorious might so that you may have great endurance and patience.

9. **Choose to serve God rather than the idols of this world.**

   Joshua 24:15 But if serving the LORD seems undesirable to you, then choose for yourselves this day whom you will serve, whether the gods your forefathers served beyond the River, or the gods of the Amorites, in whose land you are living. But as for me and my household, we will serve the LORD.

1 Kings 18:21 Elijah went before the people and said, "How long will you waver between two opinions? If the LORD is God, follow him; but if Baal is God, follow him." But the people said nothing.

Isaiah 42:8

10. God's plans will happen; he will carry them through.

Isaiah 14:24, 27 The LORD Almighty has sworn, Surely, as I have planned, so it will be, and as I have purposed, so it will stand.... For the LORD Almighty has purposed, and who can thwart him? His hand is stretched out, and who can turn it back?

Proverbs 16:9 In his heart a man plans his course, but the LORD determines his steps.

Isaiah 43:13

Questions to ask when making decisions

1. Does this activity or plan please God or sadden him?

Ephesians 4:30 And do not grieve the Holy Spirit of God, with whom you were sealed for the day of redemption.

John 8:28–29 So Jesus said,... "The one who sent me is with me; he has not left me alone, for I always do what pleases him."

2. Is this activity an act of our sinful nature or a fruit of the Spirit?

Galatians 5:16 So I say, live by the Spirit, and you will not gratify the desires of the sinful nature.

Galatians 5:17–23

3. Does this activity or plan honor God, or is it something to draw attention to yourself?

1 Corinthians 10:31 So whether you eat or drink or whatever you do, do it all for the glory of God.

Philippians 2:3 Do nothing out of selfish ambition or vain conceit, but in humility consider others better than yourselves.

4. **Would this equip you to serve Jesus better?**

   2 Timothy 2:21–22 If a man cleanses himself from the latter, he will be an instrument for noble purposes, made holy, useful to the Master and prepared to do any good work. Flee the evil desires of youth, and pursue righteousness, faith, love and peace, along with those who call on the Lord out of a pure heart.

5. **Does this activity or plan please your parents or grieve them? Is it in disobedience to them?**

   Ephesians 6:1–2 Children, obey your parents in the Lord, for this is right. "Honor your father and mother"—which is the first commandment with a promise.

   Colossians 3:20

6. **Would this activity cause others to stumble in their walk with the Lord?**

   Romans 14:21 It is better not to eat meat or drink wine or to do anything else that will cause your brother to fall.

   Matthew 18:6–7 But if anyone causes one of these little ones who believe in me to sin, it would be better for him to have a large millstone hung around his neck and to be drowned in the depths of the sea. Woe to the world because of the things that cause people to sin! Such things must come, but woe to the man through whom they come!

   1 Corinthians 8:13

7. **Does it show that you love God or that you love the world?**

   1 John 2:15–17 Do not love the world or anything in the world. If anyone loves the world, the love of the Father is not in him. For everything in the world—the cravings of sinful man, the lust of his eyes and the boasting of what he has and does—comes not from the Father but from the world. The world and its desires pass away, but the man who does the will of God lives forever.

Biblical Illustration—Abraham's servant (Genesis 24)

Church Life

See also Plan of Salvation, Spiritual Gifts

1. Meeting together as believers is not to be neglected.

Hebrews 10:24–25 And let us consider how we may spur one another on toward love and good deeds. Let us not give up meeting together, as some are in the habit of doing, but let us encourage one another—and all the more as you see the Day approaching.

Psalm 122:1 I rejoiced with those who said to me, "Let us go to the house of the LORD."

2. Submission to the authority of church leaders is required.

Hebrews 13:17 Obey your leaders and submit to their authority. They keep watch over you as men who must give an account. Obey them so that their work will be a joy, not a burden, for that would be of no advantage to you.

3. Church leaders are to be honored and esteemed.

1 Thessalonians 5:12–13 Now we ask you, brothers, to respect those who work hard among you, who are over you in the Lord and who admonish you. Hold them in the highest regard in love because of their work. Live in peace with each other.

4. Believers need each other for the body to function as God planned.

Romans 12:4–6 Just as each of us has one body with many members, and these members do not all have the same function, so in Christ we who are many form one body, and each member belongs to all the others. We have different gifts, according to the grace given us.

1 Corinthians 12:21 The eye cannot say to the hand, "I don't need you!" And the head cannot say to the feet, "I don't need you!"

1 Corinthians 12:26 If one part suffers, every part suffers with it; if one part is honored, every part rejoices with it.

1 Corinthians 12:12–18

5. **Receiving instruction from gifted individuals within the body is essential for personal growth.**

Ephesians 4:11–13 It was he who gave some to be apostles, some to be prophets, some to be evangelists, and some to be pastors and teachers, to prepare God's people for works of service, so that the body of Christ may be built up until we all reach unity in the faith and in the knowledge of the Son of God and become mature, attaining to the whole measure of the fullness of Christ.

Colossians 1:9–10, 28; 3:16

6. **Passages that encourage us in our relationships with one another are numerous.**

John 13:34–35 A new command I give you: Love one another. As I have loved you, so you must love one another. By this all men will know that you are my disciples, if you love one another.

Galatians 6:2 Carry each other's burdens, and in this way you will fulfill the law of Christ.

1 Thessalonians 5:11 Therefore encourage one another and build each other up, just as in fact you are doing.

Romans 15:7 Accept one another, then, just as Christ accepted you, in order to bring praise to God.

Ephesians 4:2 Be completely humble and gentle; be patient, bearing with one another in love.

Romans 12:10; Ephesians 4:32; 1 Thessalonians 5:15; Hebrews 3:13; James 5:16

7. **Realize that not everyone who is a member or attendee of a church is a genuine believer.**

Matthew 13:36–40 Then he left the crowd and went into the house. His disciples came to him and said, "Explain to us the parable of the weeds in the field." He answered, "The one who sowed the good seed is the Son of Man. The field is the world, and the good seed stands for the sons of the kingdom. The weeds are the sons of the evil one, and the enemy who sows them is the devil. The harvest is the end of the age, and the harvesters are angels. As the weeds are pulled up and burned in the fire, so it will be at the end of the age."

2 Peter 2:1 But there were also false prophets among the people, just as there will be false teachers among you. They will secretly introduce destructive heresies, even denying the sovereign Lord who bought them—bringing swift destruction on themselves.

Matthew 15:8–9

Biblical Illustrations—Matthew 13

Compassion

See also Attitude, Selfishness

1. God's compassion for us is evident.

Psalm 116:5 The LORD is gracious and righteous; our God is full of compassion.

Lamentations 3:21–23 Yet this I call to mind and therefore I have hope: Because of the LORD's great love we are not consumed, for his compassions never fail. They are new every morning; great is your faithfulness.

Micah 7:18–19 Who is a God like you, who pardons sin and forgives the transgression of the remnant of his inheritance? You do not stay angry forever but delight to show mercy. You will again have compassion on us; you will tread our sins underfoot and hurl all our iniquities into the depths of the sea.

2. We should have compassion for others.

Proverbs 29:7 The righteous care about justice for the poor, but the wicked have no such concern.

Zechariah 7:9–10 This is what the LORD Almighty says: "Administer true justice; show mercy and compassion to one another. Do not oppress the widow or the fatherless, the alien or the poor. In your hearts do not think evil of each other."

Colossians 3:12–13 Therefore, as God's chosen people, holy and dearly loved, clothe yourselves with compassion, kindness, humility, gentleness and patience. Bear with each other and forgive whatever grievances you may have against one another. Forgive as the Lord forgave you.

1 John 3:17–18 If anyone has material possessions and sees his brother in need but has no pity on him, how can the love of God be in him? Dear children, let us not love with words or tongue but with actions and in truth.

James 2:15–16

Biblical Illustrations—David to Saul (1 Samuel 23:21); David to Mephibosheth (2 Samuel 9); Jonah (Jonah 4); Jesus (Matthew 14:14; 15:32; 20:34; Mark 1:40–42); Good Samaritan (Luke 10)

Complaining/Critical Spirit

See also Attitude, Bitterness, Contentment

1. **A spirit of complaining is not to be part of a Christian's walk.**

   Philippians 2:14–15 Do everything without complaining or arguing, so that you may become blameless and pure, children of God without fault in a crooked and depraved generation, in which you shine like stars in the universe.

   James 5:9 Don't grumble against each other, brothers, or you will be judged. The Judge is standing at the door!

   1 Corinthians 10:10; Colossians 3:13

2. **Let your outlook and manner be that of patient acceptance.**

   Ecclesiastes 7:8–9 The end of a matter is better than its beginning, and patience is better than pride. Do not be quickly provoked in your spirit, for anger resides in the lap of fools.

   Romans 15:7 Accept one another, then, just as Christ accepted you, in order to bring praise to God.

   Ephesians 4:2 Be completely humble and gentle; be patient, bearing with one another in love.

   Psalm 40:1; 2 Corinthians 6:6; Galatians 5:22

3. **Christ's peace and contentment are vital ingredients for a positive spirit.**

   John 14:27 Peace I leave with you; my peace I give you. I do not give to you as the world gives. Do not let your hearts be troubled and do not be afraid.

Philippians 4:11–13 I am not saying this because I am in need, for I have learned to be content whatever the circumstances. I know what it is to be in need, and I know what it is to have plenty. I have learned the secret of being content in any and every situation, whether well fed or hungry, whether living in plenty or in want. I can do everything through him who gives me strength.

Colossians 3:12–13 Therefore, as God's chosen people, holy and dearly loved, clothe yourselves with compassion, kindness, humility, gentleness and patience. Bear with each other and forgive whatever grievances you may have against one another. Forgive as the Lord forgave you.

Biblical Illustration—Israel (Exodus 16; Numbers 16)

Confession/Repentance

See also Forgiveness, Guilt

1. Confession of sin is necessary for our total well-being.

Psalm 32:5 Then I acknowledged my sin to you and did not cover up my iniquity. I said, "I will confess my transgressions to the LORD"—and you forgave the guilt of my sin.

Psalm 41:4 I said, "O LORD, have mercy on me; heal me, for I have sinned against you."

Psalm 38:18 I confess my iniquity; I am troubled by my sin.

Ezra 10:11; Psalm 25:11; 51:7

2. Repentance and confession lead to restoration and healing.

1 John 1:9 If we confess our sins, he is faithful and just and will forgive us our sins and purify us from all unrighteousness.

Psalm 51:9–12 Hide your face from my sins and blot out all my iniquity. Create in me a pure heart, O God, and renew a steadfast spirit within me. Do not cast me from your presence or take your Holy Spirit from me. Restore to me the joy of your salvation and grant me a willing spirit, to sustain me.

Romans 4:7–8 Blessed are they whose transgressions are forgiven, whose sins are covered. Blessed is the man whose sin the Lord will never count against him.

2 Corinthians 5:17

3. Confession of sin involves a commitment to turn from that sin.

Proverbs 28:13 He who conceals his sins does not prosper, but whoever confesses and renounces them finds mercy.

Isaiah 1:16 Wash and make yourselves clean. Take your evil deeds out of my sight! Stop doing wrong.

Ezekiel 18:30–31 Therefore, O house of Israel, I will judge you, each one according to his ways, declares the Sovereign LORD. Repent! Turn away from all your offenses; then sin will not be your downfall. Rid yourselves of all the offenses you have committed, and get a new heart and a new spirit. Why will you die, O house of Israel?

Isaiah 55:6–7; Ephesians 4:22–24

4. Confession of sin may require restitution.

Proverbs 14:9 Fools mock at making amends for sin, but goodwill is found among the upright.

Luke 19:8 But Zacchaeus stood up and said to the Lord, "Look, Lord! Here and now I give half of my possessions to the poor, and if I have cheated anybody out of anything, I will pay back four times the amount."

Biblical Illustrations—David (Psalm 51); Christians at Ephesus (Acts 19:18–19); Israelites under the law (Leviticus 6:1–5; Numbers 5:6–7)

Contentment

See also Complaining, Jealousy, Materialism

1. Contentment is enjoying God no matter what the circumstances.

Psalm 84:10–11 Better is one day in your courts than a thousand elsewhere; I would rather be a doorkeeper in the house of my God than dwell in the tents of the wicked. For the Lord God is a sun and shield; the Lord bestows favor and honor; no good thing does he withhold from those whose walk is blameless.

Philippians 4:11–13 I am not saying this because I am in need, for I have learned to be content whatever the circumstances. I know what it is to be in need, and I know what it is to have plenty. I have learned the secret of being content in any and every situation, whether well fed or hungry, whether living in plenty or in want. I can do everything through him who gives me strength.

2. Contentment with material possessions is required.

Hebrews 13:5 Keep your lives free from the love of money and be content with what you have, because God has said, "Never will I leave you; never will I forsake you."

1 Timothy 6:6–8 But godliness with contentment is great gain. For we brought nothing into the world, and we can take nothing out of it. But if we have food and clothing, we will be content with that.

Proverbs 16:8; 17:1; Ecclesiastes 2:24

3. Contentment is possible, even when others are prosperous.

Psalm 73:2–3, 16–17, 25–26 But as for me, my feet had almost slipped; I had nearly lost my foothold. For I envied the arrogant when

I saw the prosperity of the wicked. . . . When I tried to understand all this, it was oppressive to me till I entered the sanctuary of God; then I understood their final destiny. . . . Whom have I in heaven but you? And earth has nothing I desire besides you. My flesh and my heart may fail, but God is the strength of my heart and my portion forever.

Psalm 37:7, 16 Be still before the LORD and wait patiently for him; do not fret when men succeed in their ways, when they carry out their wicked schemes. . . . Better the little that the righteous have than the wealth of many wicked.

Proverbs 15:16–17

4. Contentment means we will be thankful for what we have in the Lord.

Psalm 107:8–9 Let them give thanks to the LORD for his unfailing love and his wonderful deeds for men, for he satisfies the thirsty and fills the hungry with good things.

Psalm 100:4–5 Enter his gates with thanksgiving and his courts with praise; give thanks to him and praise his name. For the LORD is good and his love endures forever; his faithfulness continues through all generations.

Cross-Dressing

See also Choices, Sexual Purity

1. God views transvestite activity (cross-dressing) as detestable behavior.

Deuteronomy 22:5 A woman must not wear men's clothing, nor a man wear women's clothing, for the LORD your God detests anyone who does this.

Leviticus 20:23 You must not live according to the customs of the nations I am going to drive out before you. Because they did all these things, I abhorred them.

2. Separation from such sinful behavior is required by God.

Ephesians 5:11–12 Have nothing to do with the fruitless deeds of darkness, but rather expose them. For it is shameful even to mention what the disobedient do in secret.

2 Corinthians 6:17–18 Therefore come out from them and be separate, says the Lord. Touch no unclean thing, and I will receive you. I will be a Father to you, and you will be my sons and daughters, says the Lord Almighty.

Ephesians 4:17–20

3. The Christian young person must have higher standards.

Titus 2:11–12 For the grace of God that brings salvation has appeared to all men. It teaches us to say "No" to ungodliness and worldly passions, and to live self-controlled, upright and godly lives in this present age.

Titus 2:6–8 Similarly, encourage the young men to be self-controlled. In everything set them an example by doing what is good. In your teaching show integrity, seriousness and soundness of speech that cannot be condemned, so that those who oppose you may be ashamed because they have nothing bad to say about us.

Colossians 3:1–5

Dating/Courtship

See also Broken Heart, Choices, Sexual Purity, Singleness

In biblical times, selection of a mate involved parents arranging for the marriage. Today, most Western cultures involve the young adult in the decision.

1. **Finding a mate must be accomplished in accordance with God's will.**

   Psalm 37:3–4 Trust in the LORD and do good; dwell in the land and enjoy safe pasture. Delight yourself in the LORD and he will give you the desires of your heart.

   Ecclesiastes 12:1 Remember your Creator in the days of your youth, before the days of trouble come and the years approach when you will say, "I find no pleasure in them."

   Genesis 24:14; Proverbs 3:5–6

2. **There should be parental involvement and support in this decision.**

   Proverbs 6:20–24 My son, keep your father's commands and do not forsake your mother's teaching. Bind them upon your heart forever; fasten them around your neck. When you walk, they will guide you; when you sleep, they will watch over you; when you awake, they will speak to you. For these commands are a lamp, this teaching is a light, and the corrections of discipline are the way to life, keeping you from the immoral woman, from the smooth tongue of the wayward wife.

Ephesians 6:2–3 "Honor your father and mother"—which is the first commandment with a promise—that it may go well with you and that you may enjoy long life on the earth.

Proverbs 4:20–22; 5:1–2

3. **Dating or courtship for marriage should be with another believer only.**

   2 Corinthians 6:14–15 Do not be yoked together with unbelievers. For what do righteousness and wickedness have in common? Or what fellowship can light have with darkness? What harmony is there between Christ and Belial? What does a believer have in common with an unbeliever?

4. **Intermarriage with unbelievers was a major problem in the Old Testament and provides an example of what to avoid today.**

   Judges 3:6–7 They took their daughters in marriage and gave their own daughters to their sons, and served their gods. The Israelites did evil in the eyes of the LORD; they forgot the LORD their God and served the Baals and the Asherahs.

   Genesis 24:1–4; Nehemiah 13:26–27

5. **High standards and guidelines for behavior need to be in place for commitment to sexual purity.**

   Job 31:1 I made a covenant with my eyes not to look lustfully at a girl.

   2 Timothy 2:22 Flee the evil desires of youth, and pursue righteousness, faith, love and peace, along with those who call on the Lord out of a pure heart.

   1 Thessalonians 4:3–4 It is God's will that you should be sanctified: that you should avoid sexual immorality; that each of you should learn to control his own body in a way that is holy and honorable.

   1 Timothy 4:12

Biblical Illustrations—Rebekah's character qualities (Genesis 24); Boaz and Ruth (Ruth 1–4)

Death/Grief

See also Suffering, Compassion, Orphan

1. God is sovereign over death; his timing is as he planned.

Psalm 39:4–5 Show me, O LORD, my life's end and the number of my days; let me know how fleeting is my life. You have made my days a mere handbreadth; the span of my years is as nothing before you. Each man's life is but a breath.

Hebrews 9:27 Just as man is destined to die once, and after that to face judgment.

Genesis 3:19; Matthew 10:29–31

Fear of Death

1. Not even death can separate us from God and his love.

Psalm 23:4 Even though I walk through the valley of the shadow of death, I will fear no evil, for you are with me; your rod and your staff, they comfort me.

Romans 8:38–39 For I am convinced that neither death nor life, neither angels nor demons, neither the present nor the future, nor any powers, neither height nor depth, nor anything else in all creation, will be able to separate us from the love of God that is in Christ Jesus our Lord.

2. Death for the believer means being in the presence of Christ.

Philippians 1:21–23 For to me, to live is Christ and to die is gain. If I am to go on living in the body, this will mean fruitful labor for me. Yet what shall I choose? I do not know! I am torn between the two: I desire to depart and be with Christ, which is better by far.

2 Corinthians 5:6–8 Therefore we are always confident and know that as long as we are at home in the body we are away from the Lord. We live by faith, not by sight. We are confident, I say, and would prefer to be away from the body and at home with the Lord.

Isaiah 57:2; John 14:1–3

3. **Death for the believer means receiving a changed and glorified body.**

John 11:25–26 Jesus said to her, "I am the resurrection and the life. He who believes in me will live, even though he dies; and whoever lives and believes in me will never die. Do you believe this?"

Philippians 3:21 Who, by the power that enables him to bring everything under his control, will transform our lowly bodies so that they will be like his glorious body.

1 Corinthians 15:51–52 Listen, I tell you a mystery: We will not all sleep, but we will all be changed—in a flash, in the twinkling of an eye, at the last trumpet. For the trumpet will sound, the dead will be raised imperishable, and we will be changed.

John 6:40; 1 John 3:2

4. **Jesus's death brings ultimate freedom from fear of death.**

1 Peter 1:3–5 Praise be to the God and Father of our Lord Jesus Christ! In his great mercy he has given us new birth into a living hope through the resurrection of Jesus Christ from the dead, and into an inheritance that can never perish, spoil or fade—kept in heaven for you, who through faith are shielded by God's power until the coming of the salvation that is ready to be revealed in the last time.

Hebrews 2:9–15

Loss by Death

See also Broken Heart

1. David expressed his grief to God.

Psalm 31:9–10 Be merciful to me, O Lord, for I am in distress; my eyes grow weak with sorrow, my soul and my body with grief. My life is consumed by anguish and my years by groaning; my strength fails because of my affliction, and my bones grow weak.

Psalm 56:8 Record my lament; list my tears on your scroll—are they not in your record?

2. God can restore joy.

Isaiah 51:11 The ransomed of the Lord will return. They will enter Zion with singing; everlasting joy will crown their heads. Gladness and joy will overtake them, and sorrow and sighing will flee away.

3. God's presence and strength are constant.

Psalm 46:1–3, 7 God is our refuge and strength, an ever-present help in trouble. Therefore we will not fear, though the earth give way and the mountains fall into the heart of the sea, though its waters roar and foam and the mountains quake with their surging. . . . The Lord Almighty is with us; the God of Jacob is our fortress.

Lamentations 3:21–24 Yet this I call to mind and therefore I have hope: Because of the Lord's great love we are not consumed, for his compassions never fail. They are new every morning; great is your faithfulness. I say to myself, "The Lord is my portion; therefore I will wait for him."

Deuteronomy 31:6; Isaiah 26:3; 41:10

4. We must help bring comfort to those who mourn the loss of someone close.

Romans 12:15 Rejoice with those who rejoice; mourn with those who mourn.

John 11:33–36 When Jesus saw her weeping, and the Jews who had come along with her also weeping, he was deeply moved in spirit and troubled. "Where have you laid him?" he asked. "Come and see, Lord," they replied. Jesus wept. Then the Jews said, "See how he loved him!"

Matthew 5:4

5. Death will be conquered in the end.

1 Corinthians 15:26 The last enemy to be destroyed is death.

Isaiah 25:8 He will swallow up death forever. The Sovereign LORD will wipe away the tears from all faces; he will remove the disgrace of his people from all the earth. The LORD has spoken.

Revelation 21:4

Biblical Illustration—Mary and Martha (John 11)

Depression

See also Broken Heart, Self-Worth, Worry

1. Depression is a heavy burden and feels insurmountable.

Psalm 13:2 How long must I wrestle with my thoughts and every day have sorrow in my heart? How long will my enemy triumph over me?

Psalm 88:1–5 O Lord, the God who saves me, day and night I cry out before you. May my prayer come before you; turn your ear to my cry. For my soul is full of trouble and my life draws near the grave. I am counted among those who go down to the pit; I am like a man without strength. I am set apart with the dead, like the slain who lie in the grave, whom you remember no more, who are cut off from your care.

Psalm 109:22; Proverbs 18:14

2. God understands despair.

Psalm 38:9 All my longings lie open before you, O Lord; my sighing is not hidden from you.

Job 23:10 But he knows the way that I take; when he has tested me, I will come forth as gold.

Matthew 26:38 Then he said to them, "My soul is overwhelmed with sorrow to the point of death. Stay here and keep watch with me."

Psalm 18:28

3. God is the answer to a young person in despair.

Psalm 43:5 Why are you downcast, O my soul? Why so disturbed within me? Put your hope in God, for I will yet praise him, my Savior and my God.

Psalm 46:1 God is our refuge and strength, an ever-present help in trouble.

Psalm 16:11; John 14:27

4. God is big enough to keep a person from sinking further into depression.

Psalm 69:13–15 But I pray to you, O LORD, in the time of your favor; in your great love, O God, answer me with your sure salvation. Rescue me from the mire, do not let me sink; deliver me from those who hate me, from the deep waters. Do not let the floodwaters engulf me or the depths swallow me up or the pit close its mouth over me.

Isaiah 43:1–2 But now, this is what the LORD says—he who created you, O Jacob, he who formed you, O Israel: "Fear not, for I have redeemed you; I have summoned you by name; you are mine. When you pass through the waters, I will be with you; and when you pass through the rivers, they will not sweep over you. When you walk through the fire, you will not be burned; the flames will not set you ablaze."

Psalm 32:5–8

5. God provides hope and comfort.

Psalm 16:8 I have set the LORD always before me. Because he is at my right hand, I will not be shaken.

2 Corinthians 1:3–4 Praise be to the God and Father of our Lord Jesus Christ, the Father of compassion and the God of all comfort, who comforts us in all our troubles, so that we can comfort those in any trouble with the comfort we ourselves have received from God.

Ephesians 1:17–19; Hebrews 12:2

6. **Is it possible that sin is the cause of this depression? Cain was depressed because of sin in his life.**

Genesis 4:6–7 Then the LORD said to Cain, "Why are you angry? Why is your face downcast? If you do what is right, will you not be accepted? But if you do not do what is right, sin is crouching at your door; it desires to have you, but you must master it."

7. **When sin is the cause of depression, confession must take place to begin the healing process.**

Psalm 32:3–5 When I kept silent, my bones wasted away through my groaning all day long. For day and night your hand was heavy upon me; my strength was sapped as in the heat of summer. Then I acknowledged my sin to you and did not cover up my iniquity. I said, "I will confess my transgressions to the LORD"—and you forgave the guilt of my sin.

Psalm 25:17–18 The troubles of my heart have multiplied; free me from my anguish. Look upon my affliction and my distress and take away all my sins.

Psalm 51

Note: It would be beneficial to have the counselee see a physician, pastor, or trained biblical counselor.

Divorced Parents

See also Parents, Forgiving Others, Suffering, Trust

1. **Youth whose parents divorce should seek support from God, Christian friends, and leaders.**

   Isaiah 41:10 So do not fear, for I am with you; do not be dismayed, for I am your God. I will strengthen you and help you; I will uphold you with my righteous right hand.

   Psalm 42:8 By day the LORD directs his love, at night his song is with me—a prayer to the God of my life.

   Galatians 6:2 Carry each other's burdens, and in this way you will fulfill the law of Christ.

   Romans 12:15 Rejoice with those who rejoice; mourn with those who mourn.

   Psalm 27:10; 91:1–2; Isaiah 40:27–31

2. **Although divorce is not God's choice, it does happen when people harden their hearts against what he wants them to do.**

   Malachi 2:14–16 You ask, "Why?" It is because the LORD is acting as the witness between you and the wife of your youth, because you have broken faith with her, though she is your partner, the wife of your marriage covenant. Has not the LORD made them one? In flesh and spirit they are his. And why one? Because he was seeking godly offspring. So guard yourself in your spirit, and do not break faith with the wife of your youth. "I hate divorce," says the LORD God of Israel.

Mark 10:3–5 "What did Moses command you?" he replied. They said, "Moses permitted a man to write a certificate of divorce and send her away." "It was because your hearts were hard that Moses wrote you this law," Jesus replied.

3. **God does permit divorce for marital unfaithfulness and for desertion of a Christian by a non-Christian.**

   Matthew 19:9 I tell you that anyone who divorces his wife, except for marital unfaithfulness, and marries another woman commits adultery.

   1 Corinthians 7:15 But if the unbeliever leaves, let him do so. A believing man or woman is not bound in such circumstances; God has called us to live in peace.

4. **If sin is involved in the divorce, forgiveness is available.**

   1 John 1:9 If we confess our sins, he is faithful and just and will forgive us our sins and purify us from all unrighteousness.

   Psalm 130:3–4 If you, O LORD, kept a record of sins, O Lord, who could stand? But with you there is forgiveness; therefore you are feared.

   Daniel 9:9 The Lord our God is merciful and forgiving, even though we have rebelled against him.

5. **The youth must forgive his or her parents for any wrongdoings that brought about the divorce.**

   Colossians 3:13 Bear with each other and forgive whatever grievances you may have against one another. Forgive as the Lord forgave you.

   Matthew 5:23–24; Ephesians 4:32

Dress/Clothes

See also Attitude

1. **God has promised to supply our necessary clothing.**

   Matthew 6:28–30 Why do you worry about clothes? See how the lilies of the field grow. They do not labor or spin. Yet I tell you that not even Solomon in all his splendor was dressed like one of these. If that is how God clothes the grass of the field, which is here today and tomorrow is thrown into the fire, will he not much more clothe you, O you of little faith?

2. **He knows that we have need of clothing but asks that we give him priority in our lives.**

   Matthew 6:32–33 Your heavenly Father knows that you need them. But seek first his kingdom and his righteousness, and all these things will be given to you as well.

3. **People who did not put God first in their lives found no benefit from dressing even in essential clothing.**

   Haggai 1:6 You have planted much, but have harvested little. You eat, but never have enough. You drink, but never have your fill. You put on clothes, but are not warm. You earn wages, only to put them in a purse with holes in it.

4. **A godly contentment with our present possessions is a mark of Christian maturity.**

   1 Timothy 6:6–8 But godliness with contentment is great gain. For we brought nothing into the world, and we can take nothing out of it. But if we have food and clothing, we will be content with that.

Philippians 4:12 I know what it is to be in need, and I know what it is to have plenty. I have learned the secret of being content in any and every situation, whether well fed or hungry, whether living in plenty or in want.

1 Corinthians 10:14; 1 John 5:21

5. **The apostle Paul was willing to be poorly dressed for the sake of the gospel.**

1 Corinthians 4:11 To this very hour we go hungry and thirsty, we are in rags, we are brutally treated, we are homeless.

6. **God is concerned about those living in poverty without adequate clothing and expects us to be part of the solution.**

Deuteronomy 10:18–19 He defends the cause of the fatherless and the widow, and loves the alien, giving him food and clothing. And you are to love those who are aliens, for you yourselves were aliens in Egypt.

James 2:15–16 Suppose a brother or sister is without clothes and daily food. If one of you says to him, "Go, I wish you well; keep warm and well fed," but does nothing about his physical needs, what good is it?

7. **Clothes should not make a difference in our acceptance of people.**

James 2:2–4 Suppose a man comes into your meeting wearing a gold ring and fine clothes, and a poor man in shabby clothes also comes in. If you show special attention to the man wearing fine clothes and say, "Here's a good seat for you," but say to the poor man, "You stand there" or "Sit on the floor by my feet," have you not discriminated among yourselves and become judges with evil thoughts?

8. **While God would not expect that we remain dated or dowdy in our apparel, he does require modesty, good taste, and moderation. (Principles from these texts would also apply to young men.)**

1 Timothy 2:9–10 I also want women to dress modestly, with decency and propriety, not with braided hair or gold or pearls or expensive clothes, but with good deeds, appropriate for women who profess to worship God.

1 Peter 3:3–4 Your beauty should not come from outward adornment, such as braided hair and the wearing of gold jewelry and fine clothes. Instead, it should be that of your inner self, the unfading beauty of a gentle and quiet spirit, which is of great worth in God's sight.

Romans 14:13; 1 Corinthians 10:32

9. People see outward appearance; God sees the heart.

1 Samuel 16:7 But the LORD said to Samuel, "Do not consider his appearance or his height, for I have rejected him. The LORD does not look at the things man looks at. Man looks at the outward appearance, but the LORD looks at the heart."

Matthew 23:27–28

10. Spiritual qualities are the most important "clothing."

Colossians 3:12–14 Therefore, as God's chosen people, holy and dearly loved, clothe yourselves with compassion, kindness, humility, gentleness and patience. Bear with each other and forgive whatever grievances you may have against one another. Forgive as the Lord forgave you. And over all these virtues put on love, which binds them all together in perfect unity.

1 Peter 5:5 All of you, clothe yourselves with humility toward one another, because, "God opposes the proud but gives grace to the humble."

Proverbs 3:21–22

Biblical Illustrations—Sarah (1 Peter 3:1–6); women of Zion (Isaiah 3:16–26)

Drinking/Drugs

See also Choices, Temptation

1. **The Christian's body, as a temple of the Holy Spirit, should not be subjected to the harmful effects of drug and alcohol abuse.**

    1 Corinthians 6:19 Do you not know that your body is a temple of the Holy Spirit, who is in you, whom you have received from God? You are not your own.

    Ephesians 5:18 Do not get drunk on wine, which leads to debauchery. Instead, be filled with the Spirit.

    Romans 13:14

2. **Negative effects from drunkenness are evident.**

    Proverbs 29:30–35 Who has woe? Who has sorrow? Who has strife? Who has complaints? Who has needless bruises? Who has bloodshot eyes? Those who linger over wine, who go to sample bowls of mixed wine. Do not gaze at wine when it is red, when it sparkles in the cup, when it goes down smoothly! In the end it bites like a snake and poisons like a viper. Your eyes will see strange sights and your mind imagine confusing things. You will be like one sleeping on the high seas, lying on top of the rigging. "They hit me," you will say, "but I'm not hurt! They beat me, but I don't feel it! When will I wake up so I can find another drink?"

    Isaiah 28:7–8

3. **Note these associations with drunkenness that are unattractive and lead to further sin.**

    Genesis 9:21—exposure, nakedness

Job 12:25—staggering

Psalm 107:27—reeling, staggering, at wits' end

Proverbs 23:21—poverty, drowsiness

Isaiah 19:14—staggering in vomit

Isaiah 24:20—reeling, swaying, and falling

Jeremiah 25:27—vomiting

Lamentations 4:21—stripped naked

Ezekiel 23:33—ruin, desolation

Romans 13:13—indecent behavior

Ephesians 5:18—debauchery

4. **Drunken behavior is sinful and evidence of a deep spiritual problem.**

Galatians 5:19–21 The acts of the sinful nature are obvious: sexual immorality, impurity and debauchery; idolatry and witchcraft; hatred, discord, jealousy, fits of rage, selfish ambition, dissensions, factions and envy; drunkenness, orgies, and the like. I warn you, as I did before, that those who live like this will not inherit the kingdom of God.

1 Corinthians 6:9–11

5. **Drunken behavior is not acceptable behavior for the child of God.**

Isaiah 5:11–12, 22 Woe to those who rise early in the morning to run after their drinks, who stay up late at night till they are inflamed with wine. They have harps and lyres at their banquets, tambourines and flutes and wine, but they have no regard for the deeds of the LORD, no respect for the work of his hands. . . . Woe to those who are heroes at drinking wine and champions at mixing drinks.

Habakkuk 2:15–16 Woe to him who gives drink to his neighbors, pouring it from the wineskin till they are drunk, so that he can gaze on their naked bodies. You will be filled with shame instead of glory. Now it is your turn! Drink and be exposed! The cup from the LORD's right hand is coming around to you, and disgrace will cover your glory.

Proverbs 20:1; Romans 13:13–14; 1 Peter 4:1–3

6. It is God's will for people to be released from these habits.

1 Corinthians 10:13 No temptation has seized you except what is common to man. And God is faithful; he will not let you be tempted beyond what you can bear. But when you are tempted, he will also provide a way out so that you can stand up under it.

Romans 12:1–2

7. Our part is to know that Christ's death included provision for victory over sin.

Romans 6:6, 11–13 For we know that our old self was crucified with him so that the body of sin might be done away with, that we should no longer be slaves to sin. . . . In the same way, count yourselves dead to sin but alive to God in Christ Jesus. Therefore do not let sin reign in your mortal body so that you obey its evil desires. Do not offer the parts of your body to sin, as instruments of wickedness, but rather offer yourselves to God, as those who have been brought from death to life; and offer the parts of your body to him as instruments of righteousness.

[Note the "know," "count," "offer" sequence for action steps.]

John 8:36 So if the Son sets you free, you will be free indeed.

8. God's strength is available to those in great need.

Isaiah 41:10 So do not fear, for I am with you; do not be dismayed, for I am your God. I will strengthen you and help you; I will uphold you with my righteous right hand.

Philippians 4:13 I can do everything through him who gives me strength.

Isaiah 40:31

Should a Christian Drink at All?

1. Consider the stumbling block principle of Scripture.

Romans 14:21 It is better not to eat meat or drink wine or to do anything else that will cause your brother to fall.

1 Corinthians 8:13 Therefore, if what I eat causes my brother to fall into sin, I will never eat meat again, so that I will not cause him to fall.

Matthew 18:6–7

2. In light of present-day statistics of tragedies resulting from the use of alcohol, asking for wisdom is essential.

James 1:5 If any of you lacks wisdom, he should ask God, who gives generously to all without finding fault, and it will be given to him.

3. Consideration of what the authorities in your life (parents, church leaders) think about this is crucial.

Ephesians 6:1–2 Children, obey your parents in the Lord, for this is right. "Honor your father and mother"—which is the first commandment with a promise.

Hebrews 13:17 Obey your leaders and submit to their authority. They keep watch over you as men who must give an account. Obey them so that their work will be a joy, not a burden, for that would be of no advantage to you.

Biblical Illustrations—Noah (Genesis 9:18–27); Lot (Genesis 19:30–38)

Note: It would be beneficial to have the counselee see a physician, pastor, or trained biblical counselor.

Eating Struggles

See also Choices, Temptation

1. Your body is God's creation, beautiful in his sight.

Genesis 1:27 So God created man in his own image, in the image of God he created him; male and female he created them.

Psalm 139:13–14 For you created my inmost being; you knit me together in my mother's womb. I praise you because I am fearfully and wonderfully made; your works are wonderful, I know that full well.

Genesis 2:22–23

2. Your body is God's possession; he bought you with a price.

1 Corinthians 6:19–20 Do you not know that your body is a temple of the Holy Spirit, who is in you, whom you have received from God? You are not your own; you were bought at a price. Therefore honor God with your body.

1 Peter 1:18–19 For you know that it was not with perishable things such as silver or gold that you were redeemed from the empty way of life handed down to you from your forefathers, but with the precious blood of Christ, a lamb without blemish or defect.

1 Peter 2:9

3. Our trust, security, and success is not in our bodies but in God who made us as we are.

Jeremiah 17:5–7 This is what the LORD says: "Cursed is the one who trusts in man, who depends on flesh for his strength and whose heart turns away from the LORD. He will be like a bush in the wastelands; he will not see prosperity when it comes. He will dwell in the parched places of the desert, in a salt land where no one lives. But blessed is the man who trusts in the LORD, whose confidence is in him."

Zechariah 4:6

4. **Taking control of what belongs to God is sin. Focusing on self is idolatry.**

Ecclesiastes 2:25 For without him, who can eat or find enjoyment?

Matthew 15:11 What goes into a man's mouth does not make him "unclean," but what comes out of his mouth, that is what makes him "unclean."

Colossians 3:5 Put to death, therefore, whatever belongs to your earthly nature: sexual immorality, impurity, lust, evil desires and greed, which is idolatry.

1 John 1:8–9

5. **Overeating, self-indulgence, and placing self ahead of God are foolishness in God's eyes.**

Proverbs 23:20–21 Do not join those who drink too much wine or gorge themselves on meat, for drunkards and gluttons become poor, and drowsiness clothes them in rags.

Philippians 3:19 Their destiny is destruction, their god is their stomach, and their glory is in their shame. Their mind is on earthly things.

Proverbs 28:7; 30:21–22; Luke 12:19–20

6. **By an act of the will, we are to give our bodies back to God.**

Romans 12:1–2 Therefore, I urge you, brothers, in view of God's mercy, to offer your bodies as living sacrifices, holy and pleasing to God—this is your spiritual act of worship. Do not conform any longer to the pattern of this world, but be transformed by the renewing of your mind. Then you will be able to test and approve what God's will is—his good, pleasing and perfect will.

7. Changing our thinking is crucial.

Isaiah 55:7–9 Let the wicked forsake his way and the evil man his thoughts. Let him turn to the LORD, and he will have mercy on him, and to our God, for he will freely pardon. "For my thoughts are not your thoughts, neither are your ways my ways," declares the LORD. "As the heavens are higher than the earth, so are my ways higher than your ways and my thoughts than your thoughts."

Philippians 4:8–9 Finally, brothers, whatever is true, whatever is noble, whatever is right, whatever is pure, whatever is lovely, whatever is admirable—if anything is excellent or praiseworthy—think about such things. Whatever you have learned or received or heard from me, or seen in me—put it into practice. And the God of peace will be with you.

Psalm 103:1–13; Proverbs 4:20–22

8. Pray before you eat and give thanks; enjoy what you eat.

Ecclesiastes 5:18 Then I realized that it is good and proper for a man to eat and drink, and to find satisfaction in his toilsome labor under the sun during the few days of life God has given him—for this is his lot.

1 Timothy 4:4–5 For everything God created is good, and nothing is to be rejected if it is received with thanksgiving, because it is consecrated by the word of God and prayer.

Ephesians 5:29; 1 Timothy 6:17

Note: It would be beneficial to have the counselee see a physician, pastor, or trained biblical counselor.

Entertainment/Art

Dancing/Internet/Movies/Music/Reading/ Television/Video Games

See also Choices, Sexual Purity, Temptation, Fighting

1. **God is creative and beautiful and has revealed himself in such ways.**

   1 Chronicles 29:11 Yours, O Lord, is the greatness and the power and the glory and the majesty and the splendor, for everything in heaven and earth is yours. Yours, O Lord, is the kingdom; you are exalted as head over all.

   Psalm 8:1, 3–4 O Lord, our Lord, how majestic is your name in all the earth! You have set your glory above the heavens.... When I consider your heavens, the work of your fingers, the moon and the stars, which you have set in place, what is man that you are mindful of him, the son of man that you care for him?

   Psalm 27:4 One thing I ask of the Lord, this is what I seek: that I may dwell in the house of the Lord all the days of my life, to gaze upon the beauty of the Lord and to seek him in his temple.

   Psalm 145:5 They will speak of the glorious splendor of your majesty, and I will meditate on your wonderful works.

   Psalm 104; Isaiah 6:3; Revelation 4:3

2. **Music, art, literature, theater, and even the games we play are all creative, cultural expressions of the humanity the Creator has**

given us for our enjoyment and for his glory. As extensions of his image, we reflect his handiwork.

Genesis 1:27, 31 So God created man in his own image, in the image of God he created him; male and female he created them.... God saw all that he had made, and it was very good. And there was evening, and there was morning—the sixth day.

Revelation 4:11 You are worthy, our Lord and God, to receive glory and honor and power, for you created all things, and by your will they were created and have their being.

2 Corinthians 3:18; 1 Timothy 6:17

3. **As with everything God has created for good, Satan, through his worldly system, seeks to corrupt and degrade, making counterfeits.**

Ezekiel 28:17 Your heart became proud on account of your beauty, and you corrupted your wisdom because of your splendor. So I threw you to the earth; I made a spectacle of you before kings.

John 8:44 You belong to your father, the devil, and you want to carry out your father's desire. He was a murderer from the beginning, not holding to the truth, for there is no truth in him. When he lies, he speaks his native language, for he is a liar and the father of lies.

1 John 5:19 We know that we are children of God, and that the whole world is under the control of the evil one.

2 Corinthians 11:14 And no wonder, for Satan himself masquerades as an angel of light.

1 Timothy 4:1; 1 John 2:15–16

4. **As fallen, sinful people, we are naturally selfish and prone to following the pathways of this world.**

Romans 7:18–20 I know that nothing good lives in me, that is, in my sinful nature. For I have the desire to do what is good, but I cannot carry it out. For what I do is not the good I want to do; no, the evil I do not want to do—this I keep on doing. Now if I do what I do not want to do, it is no longer I who do it, but it is sin living in me that does it.

James 1:14–15

5. **With the Spirit's help, the believer must actively determine not to follow Satan's corruptions, rejecting what is unseemly and immoral.**

Galatians 5:16 So I say, live by the Spirit, and you will not gratify the desires of the sinful nature.

Deuteronomy 7:26 Do not bring a detestable thing into your house or you, like it, will be set apart for destruction. Utterly abhor and detest it, for it is set apart for destruction.

Isaiah 5:20 Woe to those who call evil good and good evil, who put darkness for light and light for darkness, who put bitter for sweet and sweet for bitter.

James 1:21 Therefore, get rid of all moral filth and the evil that is so prevalent and humbly accept the word planted in you, which can save you.

James 1:27 Religion that God our Father accepts as pure and faultless is this: to look after orphans and widows in their distress and to keep oneself from being polluted by the world.

John 17:15; Colossians 2:8; 3 John 1:11

6. **The believer must actively pursue what is right, making careful, godly decisions.**

Psalm 101:2–3 I will be careful to lead a blameless life—when will you come to me? I will walk in my house with blameless heart. I will set before my eyes no vile thing. The deeds of faithless men I hate; they will not cling to me.

2 Timothy 2:22 Flee the evil desires of youth, and pursue righteousness, faith, love and peace, along with those who call on the Lord out of a pure heart.

Joshua 24:14; Galatians 5:16; Philippians 4:8

7. **Any entertainment activity can be done excessively. Be wise in the use of your time.**

Psalm 90:12 Teach us to number our days aright, that we may gain a heart of wisdom.

Ephesians 5:15–17 Be very careful, then, how you live—not as unwise but as wise, making the most of every opportunity, because the days are evil. Therefore do not be foolish, but understand what the Lord's will is.

Titus 3:8

Failure/Success

See also Choices, Suffering

1. God's view of success is our personal knowledge of him.

Jeremiah 9:23–24 This is what the LORD says: "Let not the wise man boast of his wisdom or the strong man boast of his strength or the rich man boast of his riches, but let him who boasts boast about this: that he understands and knows me, that I am the LORD, who exercises kindness, justice and righteousness on earth, for in these I delight," declares the LORD.

Psalm 73:25–26 Whom have I in heaven but you? And earth has nothing I desire besides you. My flesh and my heart may fail, but God is the strength of my heart and my portion forever.

2. Success is found in knowing and doing God's will.

Joshua 1:8–9 Do not let this Book of the Law depart from your mouth; meditate on it day and night, so that you may be careful to do everything written in it. Then you will be prosperous and successful. Have I not commanded you? Be strong and courageous. Do not be terrified; do not be discouraged, for the LORD your God will be with you wherever you go.

Micah 6:8 He has showed you, O man, what is good. And what does the LORD require of you? To act justly and to love mercy and to walk humbly with your God.

3. Though we sometimes fail, God will not fail us.

Lamentations 3:22–23 Because of the LORD's great love we are not consumed, for his compassions never fail. They are new every morning; great is your faithfulness.

Deuteronomy 31:6 Be strong and courageous. Do not be afraid or terrified because of them, for the LORD your God goes with you; he will never leave you nor forsake you.

1 Thessalonians 5:24 The one who calls you is faithful and he will do it.

Joshua 21:45

4. Our weakness is God's strength.

2 Corinthians 12:9–10 But he said to me, "My grace is sufficient for you, for my power is made perfect in weakness." Therefore I will boast all the more gladly about my weaknesses, so that Christ's power may rest on me. That is why, for Christ's sake, I delight in weaknesses, in insults, in hardships, in persecutions, in difficulties. For when I am weak, then I am strong.

Isaiah 40:28–31

5. When we feel like a failure, God wants us to keep on working and improving.

2 Timothy 1:6–7 For this reason I remind you to fan into flame the gift of God, which is in you through the laying on of my hands. For God did not give us a spirit of timidity, but a spirit of power, of love and of self-discipline.

Biblical Illustrations—Peter (John 18:15–27; 21:15–19; Acts 2); John Mark (Acts 15:36–40; 2 Timothy 4:11); Timothy (2 Timothy 1–2)

Fear/Safety/Terrorism

See also Death, Trust, Worry

1. God is the answer to a fearful heart.

Psalm 34:4 I sought the LORD, and he answered me; he delivered me from all my fears.

1 Peter 5:7 Cast all your anxiety on him because he cares for you.

Joshua 1:6–9; Job 23:8–10

2. Focus not on fear but on what is real and true.

Psalm 4:8 I will lie down and sleep in peace, for you alone, O LORD, make me dwell in safety.

Philippians 4:8 Finally, brothers, whatever is true, whatever is noble, whatever is right, whatever is pure, whatever is lovely, whatever is admirable—if anything is excellent or praiseworthy—think about such things.

Philippians 4:13

3. God is present with us in every situation.

Deuteronomy 31:8 The LORD himself goes before you and will be with you; he will never leave you nor forsake you. Do not be afraid; do not be discouraged.

Isaiah 41:10 So do not fear, for I am with you; do not be dismayed, for I am your God. I will strengthen you and help you; I will uphold you with my righteous right hand.

Psalm 73:23–24

4. Not placing ourselves in dangerous situations requires making good choices.

See Choices

5. We must not fear the past or the future.

Isaiah 43:18–19 Forget the former things; do not dwell on the past. See, I am doing a new thing! Now it springs up; do you not perceive it? I am making a way in the desert and streams in the wasteland.

Philippians 3:13–14 Forgetting what is behind and straining toward what is ahead, I press on toward the goal to win the prize for which God has called me heavenward in Christ Jesus.

Proverbs 3:5–6; Lamentations 3:21–23; Matthew 6:34

6. If there is a fear problem, there is also a love problem.

1 John 4:18 There is no fear in love. But perfect love drives out fear, because fear has to do with punishment. The one who fears is not made perfect in love.

7. God's provision of everyday needs makes fear unnecessary.

Philippians 4:19 And my God will meet all your needs according to his glorious riches in Christ Jesus.

Matthew 6:31–33 So do not worry, saying, "What shall we eat?" or "What shall we drink?" or "What shall we wear?" For the pagans run after all these things, and your heavenly Father knows that you need them. But seek first his kingdom and his righteousness, and all these things will be given to you as well.

8. God is more powerful than our enemies.

Romans 8:31 What, then, shall we say in response to this? If God is for us, who can be against us?

Psalm 27:1–3 The LORD is my light and my salvation—whom shall I fear? The LORD is the stronghold of my life—of whom shall I be afraid? When evil men advance against me to devour my flesh, when my enemies and my foes attack me, they will stumble and fall.

Though an army besiege me, my heart will not fear; though war break out against me, even then will I be confident.

Psalm 56:11; 91:4

9. We must trust God completely, even though bad things happen.

Habakkuk 3:16–19 I heard and my heart pounded, my lips quivered at the sound; decay crept into my bones, and my legs trembled. Yet I will wait patiently for the day of calamity to come on the nation invading us. Though the fig tree does not bud and there are no grapes on the vines, though the olive crop fails and the fields produce no food, though there are no sheep in the pen and no cattle in the stalls, yet I will rejoice in the LORD, I will be joyful in God my Savior. The Sovereign LORD is my strength; he makes my feet like the feet of a deer, he enables me to go on the heights.

10. God triumphs over evil in the end, and believers will be safe with the Father in heaven.

2 Thessalonians 1:6–8 God is just: He will pay back trouble to those who trouble you and give relief to you who are troubled, and to us as well. This will happen when the Lord Jesus is revealed from heaven in blazing fire with his powerful angels. He will punish those who do not know God and do not obey the gospel of our Lord Jesus.

Jude 1:14–15; Revelation 19:11–16

Biblical Illustrations—servant of Elisha (2 Kings 6:15–17); Hezekiah (2 Chronicles 32:7–8); Psalms 27; 34; 37; 46; 91; book of Habakkuk

Fighting/Violence

See also Anger, Gangs, Peer Pressure

1. Violence is not pleasing to God.

Proverbs 20:3 It is to a man's honor to avoid strife, but every fool is quick to quarrel.

Psalm 7:15–16 He who digs a hole and scoops it out falls into the pit he has made. The trouble he causes recoils on himself; his violence comes down on his own head.

Psalm 11:5 The LORD examines the righteous, but the wicked and those who love violence his soul hates.

2. Stay away from people who pick fights.

Proverbs 16:29 A violent man entices his neighbor and leads him down a path that is not good.

Proverbs 24:1–2 Do not envy wicked men, do not desire their company; for their hearts plot violence, and their lips talk about making trouble.

Titus 3:10–11 Warn a divisive person once, and then warn him a second time. After that, have nothing to do with him. You may be sure that such a man is warped and sinful; he is self-condemned.

2 Timothy 2:22–24 Flee the evil desires of youth, and pursue righteousness, faith, love and peace, along with those who call on the Lord out of a pure heart. Don't have anything to do with foolish and stupid arguments, because you know they produce quarrels. And the Lord's servant must not quarrel; instead, he must be kind to everyone, able to teach, not resentful.

Proverbs 3:31

3. **Defend yourself only if you face bodily harm or if your life is in danger. Jesus used the concept of a man defending his household, and Paul, that of a soldier on duty.**

Matthew 5:38–41 You have heard that it was said, "Eye for eye, and tooth for tooth." But I tell you, Do not resist an evil person. If someone strikes you on the right cheek, turn to him the other also. And if someone wants to sue you and take your tunic, let him have your cloak as well. If someone forces you to go one mile, go with him two miles.

Luke 11:21–22 When a strong man, fully armed, guards his own house, his possessions are safe. But when someone stronger attacks and overpowers him, he takes away the armor in which the man trusted and divides up the spoils.

Luke 12:39; 2 Timothy 2:3–4

4. **Seek help and support from those in authority (parents, school, government).**

Acts 23:16–17 But when the son of Paul's sister heard of this plot, he went into the barracks and told Paul. Then Paul called one of the centurions and said, "Take this young man to the commander; he has something to tell him."

Romans 13:3–4 For rulers hold no terror for those who do right, but for those who do wrong. Do you want to be free from fear of the one in authority? Then do what is right and he will commend you. For he is God's servant to do you good. But if you do wrong, be afraid, for he does not bear the sword for nothing. He is God's servant, an agent of wrath to bring punishment on the wrongdoer.

Acts 23; Titus 3:1–2

5. **If possible, help people in trouble.**

Jeremiah 22:3 This is what the LORD says: Do what is just and right. Rescue from the hand of his oppressor the one who has been robbed. Do no wrong or violence to the alien, the fatherless or the widow, and do not shed innocent blood in this place.

Proverbs 31:9 Speak up and judge fairly; defend the rights of the poor and needy.

Isaiah 1:17 Learn to do right! Seek justice, encourage the oppressed. Defend the cause of the fatherless, plead the case of the widow.

6. Remember that God is the ultimate defender.

Psalm 35:1 Contend, O LORD, with those who contend with me; fight against those who fight against me.

Isaiah 25:4 You have been a refuge for the poor, a refuge for the needy in his distress, a shelter from the storm and a shade from the heat. For the breath of the ruthless is like a storm driving against a wall.

Psalm 37:7; 59:16

Biblical Illustrations—Jesus at his trial (1 Peter 2:21–24); Paul's nephew (Acts 23:12–35)

Flirting

See also Dress, Lust, Sexual Purity

1. **Smooth and seductive speech is to be avoided.**

    Proverbs 2:16–17 It [wisdom] will save you also from the adulteress, from the wayward wife with her seductive words, who has left the partner of her youth and ignored the covenant she made before God.

    2 Peter 2:18 For they mouth empty, boastful words and, by appealing to the lustful desires of sinful human nature, they entice people who are just escaping from those who live in error.

    Romans 16:17–18; Ephesians 4:29–30; 5:4

2. **Flirtatious or seductive body language is not pleasing to God and could bring his discipline.**

    Proverbs 10:10 He who winks maliciously causes grief, and a chattering fool comes to ruin.

    Isaiah 3:16–17 The LORD says, "The women of Zion are haughty, walking along with outstretched necks, flirting with their eyes, tripping along with mincing steps, with ornaments jingling on their ankles. Therefore the Lord will bring sores on the heads of the women of Zion; the LORD will make their scalps bald."

3. **Dressing in a sensual and flirtatious manner is to be avoided because it could lead to great sin.**

    1 Timothy 2:9–10 I also want women to dress modestly, with decency and propriety, not with braided hair or gold or pearls or expensive clothes, but with good deeds, appropriate for women who profess to worship God.

    Ezekiel 16:15–17

4. Flirting may cause others to stumble into sin.

Matthew 18:7 Woe to the world because of the things that cause people to sin! Such things must come, but woe to the man through whom they come!

Romans 14:13, 21 Therefore let us stop passing judgment on one another. Instead, make up your mind not to put any stumbling block or obstacle in your brother's way. . . . It is better not to eat meat or drink wine or to do anything else that will cause your brother to fall.

2 Corinthians 6:3 We put no stumbling block in anyone's path, so that our ministry will not be discredited.

Luke 17:1

5. Flirtatious behavior could open our lives to Satan's schemes and enhance his desire to make us fall.

Proverbs 9:13–18 The woman Folly is loud; she is undisciplined and without knowledge. She sits at the door of her house, on a seat at the highest point of the city, calling out to those who pass by, who go straight on their way. "Let all who are simple come in here!" she says to those who lack judgment. "Stolen water is sweet; food eaten in secret is delicious!" But little do they know that the dead are there, that her guests are in the depths of the grave.

1 Peter 5:8 Be self-controlled and alert. Your enemy the devil prowls around like a roaring lion looking for someone to devour.

2 Corinthians 11:3; Ephesians 6:11–13

Biblical Illustration—Proverbs 5

Forgiveness

See also Confession, Guilt

1. There is no sin that God will not forgive.

Daniel 9:9 The Lord our God is merciful and forgiving, even though we have rebelled against him.

Psalm 86:5 You are forgiving and good, O Lord, abounding in love to all who call to you.

Romans 8:1–2 Therefore, there is now no condemnation for those who are in Christ Jesus, because through Christ Jesus the law of the Spirit of life set me free from the law of sin and death.

Psalm 130:3–4; Isaiah 44:22; Lamentations 3:22; Colossians 1:13

2. Forgiveness provided by our heavenly Father is complete.

Isaiah 38:17 Surely it was for my benefit that I suffered such anguish. In your love you kept me from the pit of destruction; you have put all my sins behind your back.

Isaiah 43:25 I, even I, am he who blots out your transgressions, for my own sake, and remembers your sins no more.

Psalm 103:12 As far as the east is from the west, so far has he removed our transgressions from us.

Micah 7:18–19

3. Asking God to forgive us is required.

1 John 1:9 If we confess our sins, he is faithful and just and will forgive us our sins and purify us from all unrighteousness.

Psalm 66:18 If I had cherished sin in my heart, the Lord would not have listened.

4. God will supply complete restoration.

Psalm 25:7 Remember not the sins of my youth and my rebellious ways; according to your love remember me, for you are good, O Lord.

2 Corinthians 5:17 Therefore, if anyone is in Christ, he is a new creation; the old has gone, the new has come!

Note: No place in Scripture does it mention we are to "forgive" ourselves.

Forgiving Others

See also Bitterness, Guilt, Confession

1. **Forgiving others is not an option; it is a command of Scripture.**

   Colossians 3:12–13 Therefore, as God's chosen people, holy and dearly loved, clothe yourselves with compassion, kindness, humility, gentleness and patience. Bear with each other and forgive whatever grievances you may have against one another. Forgive as the Lord forgave you.

   Matthew 6:9–15 This, then, is how you should pray: "Our Father in heaven, hallowed be your name, your kingdom come, your will be done on earth as it is in heaven. Give us today our daily bread. Forgive us our debts, as we also have forgiven our debtors. And lead us not into temptation, but deliver us from the evil one." For if you forgive men when they sin against you, your heavenly Father will also forgive you. But if you do not forgive men their sins, your Father will not forgive your sins.

   Matthew 5:23–24; Ephesians 4:32

2. **There is no limit to the number of times we are to forgive someone.**

   Luke 17:3–4 So watch yourselves. If your brother sins, rebuke him, and if he repents, forgive him. If he sins against you seven times in a day, and seven times comes back to you and says, "I repent," forgive him.

   Matthew 18:21–22 Then Peter came to Jesus and asked, "Lord, how many times shall I forgive my brother when he sins against me?

Up to seven times?" Jesus answered, "I tell you, not seven times, but seventy-seven times."

3. God's offer of forgiveness to anyone who asks is a great example to us.

Psalm 130:3–4 If you, O LORD, kept a record of sins, O Lord, who could stand? But with you there is forgiveness; therefore you are feared.

Romans 8:1–2 Therefore, there is now no condemnation for those who are in Christ Jesus, because through Christ Jesus the law of the Spirit of life set me free from the law of sin and death.

Micah 7:18–19 Who is a God like you, who pardons sin and forgives the transgression of the remnant of his inheritance? You do not stay angry forever but delight to show mercy. You will again have compassion on us; you will tread our sins underfoot and hurl all our iniquities into the depths of the sea.

Biblical Illustrations—parable (Matthew 18:23–35); Jesus on the cross (Luke 23:34); Stephen (Acts 7:60); Philemon

Friends

See also Choices, Forgiving Others, Peer Pressure

1. Quality friends will help and encourage us.

Proverbs 17:17 A friend loves at all times, and a brother is born for adversity.

Proverbs 27:17 As iron sharpens iron, so one man sharpens another.

Ecclesiastes 4:9–12 Two are better than one, because they have a good return for their work: If one falls down, his friend can help him up. But pity the man who falls and has no one to help him up! Also, if two lie down together, they will keep warm. But how can one keep warm alone? Though one may be overpowered, two can defend themselves. A cord of three strands is not quickly broken.

1 Thessalonians 5:11 Therefore encourage one another and build each other up, just as in fact you are doing.

Ephesians 4:2 Be completely humble and gentle; be patient, bearing with one another in love.

Proverbs 27:6; Romans 12:10; Galatians 6:2; Hebrews 10:24–25

2. Discretion in the choice of friends is important.

Psalm 119:63 I am a friend to all who fear you, to all who follow your precepts.

Proverbs 12:26 A righteous man is cautious in friendship, but the way of the wicked leads them astray.

Proverbs 22:24–25 Do not make friends with a hot-tempered man, do not associate with one easily angered, or you may learn his ways and get yourself ensnared.

Exodus 23:2 Do not follow the crowd in doing wrong. When you give testimony in a lawsuit, do not pervert justice by siding with the crowd.

1 Corinthians 15:33–34 Do not be misled: "Bad company corrupts good character." Come back to your senses as you ought, and stop sinning; for there are some who are ignorant of God—I say this to your shame.

Psalm 1:1; Proverbs 1:10; 2:11–15; 13:20; 18:24; 23:20

3. A good friend is willing to experience loss.

John 15:13 Greater love has no one than this, that he lay down his life for his friends.

Philippians 2:3–8 Do nothing out of selfish ambition or vain conceit, but in humility consider others better than yourselves. Each of you should look not only to your own interests, but also to the interests of others. Your attitude should be the same as that of Christ Jesus: Who, being in very nature God, did not consider equality with God something to be grasped, but made himself nothing, taking the very nature of a servant, being made in human likeness. And being found in appearance as a man, he humbled himself and became obedient to death—even death on a cross!

4. Restoring a friendship.

Proverbs 19:11 A man's wisdom gives him patience; it is to his glory to overlook an offense.

Ephesians 4:32 Be kind and compassionate to one another, forgiving each other, just as in Christ God forgave you.

Romans 12:18 If it is possible, as far as it depends on you, live at peace with everyone.

1 Thessalonians 5:15 Make sure that nobody pays back wrong for wrong, but always try to be kind to each other and to everyone else.

Matthew 5:23–24; Romans 15:7

Biblical Illustrations—God and Abraham (2 Chronicles 20:7; James 2:23); David and Jonathan; Paul and Timothy

Future Plans

See also Career, Fear, Choices

1. **When we acknowledge God in all of our plans, his guidance is guaranteed.**

   Psalm 143:8 Let the morning bring me word of your unfailing love, for I have put my trust in you. Show me the way I should go, for to you I lift up my soul.

   Proverbs 3:5–6 Trust in the LORD with all your heart and lean not on your own understanding; in all your ways acknowledge him, and he will make your paths straight.

2. **We must seek his will in all our plans for the future.**

   Psalm 143:10 Teach me to do your will, for you are my God; may your good Spirit lead me on level ground.

   James 4:13–15 Now listen, you who say, "Today or tomorrow we will go to this or that city, spend a year there, carry on business and make money." Why, you do not even know what will happen tomorrow. What is your life? You are a mist that appears for a little while and then vanishes. Instead, you ought to say, "If it is the Lord's will, we will live and do this or that."

   Romans 15:32 So that by God's will I may come to you with joy and together with you be refreshed.

   1 Corinthians 16:7

3. God has promised to see us through to the end.

Philippians 1:6 Being confident of this, that he who began a good work in you will carry it on to completion until the day of Christ Jesus.

Jeremiah 32:17 Ah, Sovereign LORD, you have made the heavens and the earth by your great power and outstretched arm. Nothing is too hard for you.

4. Worrying about tomorrow is unnecessary for those who seek God first.

Matthew 6:33–34 But seek first his kingdom and his righteousness, and all these things will be given to you as well. Therefore do not worry about tomorrow, for tomorrow will worry about itself. Each day has enough trouble of its own.

1 Corinthians 2:9 However, as it is written: "No eye has seen, no ear has heard, no mind has conceived what God has prepared for those who love him."

5. God's plans are the best plans.

Jeremiah 29:11–12 "For I know the plans I have for you," declares the LORD, "plans to prosper you and not to harm you, plans to give you hope and a future. Then you will call upon me and come and pray to me, and I will listen to you."

Gambling

See also Materialism, Contentment, Money

1. Gambling is deceitful and can be a trap.

Psalm 64:2, 5–6 Hide me from the conspiracy of the wicked, from that noisy crowd of evildoers. . . . They encourage each other in evil plans, they talk about hiding their snares; they say, "Who will see them?" They plot injustice and say, "We have devised a perfect plan!" Surely the mind and heart of man are cunning.

Romans 16:18 For such people are not serving our Lord Christ, but their own appetites. By smooth talk and flattery they deceive the minds of naive people.

1 Timothy 6:9–11 People who want to get rich fall into temptation and a trap and into many foolish and harmful desires that plunge men into ruin and destruction. For the love of money is a root of all kinds of evil. Some people, eager for money, have wandered from the faith and pierced themselves with many griefs. But you, man of God, flee from all this, and pursue righteousness, godliness, faith, love, endurance and gentleness.

Ephesians 4:22

2. Gambling is not good stewardship.

Luke 12:42–44 The Lord answered, "Who then is the faithful and wise manager, whom the master puts in charge of his servants to give them their food allowance at the proper time? It will be good for that servant whom the master finds doing so when he returns. I tell you the truth, he will put him in charge of all his possessions."

1 Corinthians 4:1–2 So then, men ought to regard us as servants of Christ and as those entrusted with the secret things of God. Now it is required that those who have been given a trust must prove faithful.

1 Peter 4:10 Each one should use whatever gift he has received to serve others, faithfully administering God's grace in its various forms.

3. God can and will supply all our needs financially.

Philippians 4:19 And my God will meet all your needs according to his glorious riches in Christ Jesus.

Matthew 6:33–34 But seek first his kingdom and his righteousness, and all these things will be given to you as well. Therefore do not worry about tomorrow, for tomorrow will worry about itself. Each day has enough trouble of its own.

Jeremiah 32:17

Biblical Illustration—Paul's contentment (Philippians 4)

Gangs/Bullies

See Fighting, Peer Pressure

1. Gangs of violence are on a pathway to destruction.

1 Corinthians 15:33 Do not be misled: "Bad company corrupts good character."

Proverbs 4:14–17 Do not set foot on the path of the wicked or walk in the way of evil men. Avoid it, do not travel on it; turn from it and go on your way. For they cannot sleep till they do evil; they are robbed of slumber till they make someone fall. They eat the bread of wickedness and drink the wine of violence.

Psalm 64:5–6 They encourage each other in evil plans, they talk about hiding their snares; they say, "Who will see them?" They plot injustice and say, "We have devised a perfect plan!" Surely the mind and heart of man are cunning.

Psalm 55:9–11 Confuse the wicked, O Lord, confound their speech, for I see violence and strife in the city. Day and night they prowl about on its walls; malice and abuse are within it. Destructive forces are at work in the city; threats and lies never leave its streets.

Psalm 37:12–13

2. Those who face bullies can depend on God's presence and help.

Psalm 10:12–14 Arise, LORD! Lift up your hand, O God. Do not forget the helpless. Why does the wicked man revile God? Why does he say to himself, "He won't call me to account"? But you, O God, do see trouble and grief; you consider it to take it in hand. The victim commits himself to you; you are the helper of the fatherless.

Psalm 12:7–8 O LORD, you will keep us safe and protect us from such people forever. The wicked freely strut about when what is vile is honored among men.

Psalm 31:4 Free me from the trap that is set for me, for you are my refuge.

Psalm 31:15; Proverbs 16:6

3. Guidelines from Proverbs.

Proverbs 1:10 My son, if sinners entice you, do not give in to them.

Proverbs 2:12–15 Wisdom will save you from the ways of wicked men, from men whose words are perverse, who leave the straight paths to walk in dark ways, who delight in doing wrong and rejoice in the perverseness of evil, whose paths are crooked and who are devious in their ways.

Proverbs 14:15–16 A simple man believes anything, but a prudent man gives thought to his steps. A wise man fears the LORD and shuns evil, but a fool is hotheaded and reckless.

Proverbs 15:1

4. Do what you can do to defuse the situation; let God handle the result.

Romans 12:17–21 Do not repay anyone evil for evil. Be careful to do what is right in the eyes of everybody. If it is possible, as far as it depends on you, live at peace with everyone. Do not take revenge, my friends, but leave room for God's wrath, for it is written: "It is mine to avenge; I will repay," says the Lord. On the contrary: "If your enemy is hungry, feed him; if he is thirsty, give him something to drink. In doing this, you will heap burning coals on his head." Do not be overcome by evil, but overcome evil with good.

5. Seek help and support from those in authority (parents, school, government).

Acts 23:16–17 But when the son of Paul's sister heard of this plot, he went into the barracks and told Paul. Then Paul called one of the centurions and said, "Take this young man to the commander; he has something to tell him."

Romans 13:3–4 For rulers hold no terror for those who do right, but for those who do wrong. Do you want to be free from fear of the one in authority? Then do what is right and he will commend you. For he is God's servant to do you good. But if you do wrong, be afraid, for he does not bear the sword for nothing. He is God's servant, an agent of wrath to bring punishment on the wrongdoer.

6. Christians can expect persecution.

Matthew 5:10–12 Blessed are those who are persecuted because of righteousness, for theirs is the kingdom of heaven. Blessed are you when people insult you, persecute you and falsely say all kinds of evil against you because of me. Rejoice and be glad, because great is your reward in heaven, for in the same way they persecuted the prophets who were before you.

1 John 3:13 Do not be surprised, my brothers, if the world hates you.

1 Peter 3:14–15 But even if you should suffer for what is right, you are blessed. "Do not fear what they fear; do not be frightened." But in your hearts set apart Christ as Lord. Always be prepared to give an answer to everyone who asks you to give the reason for the hope that you have. But do this with gentleness and respect.

1 Peter 2:20

Guilt

See also Confession, Forgiveness

1. **Guilt is the result of sin. As Christians, we need to agree with God: sin is sin.**

   Psalm 32:3–5 When I kept silent, my bones wasted away through my groaning all day long. For day and night your hand was heavy upon me; my strength was sapped as in the heat of summer. Then I acknowledged my sin to you and did not cover up my iniquity. I said, "I will confess my transgressions to the LORD"—and you forgave the guilt of my sin.

   Psalm 69:5 You know my folly, O God; my guilt is not hidden from you.

2. **We need to admit our sin and seek forgiveness, turning and going in the opposite direction of that sin.**

   1 John 1:8–10 If we claim to be without sin, we deceive ourselves and the truth is not in us. If we confess our sins, he is faithful and just and will forgive us our sins and purify us from all unrighteousness. If we claim we have not sinned, we make him out to be a liar and his word has no place in our lives.

   Hebrews 10:22–23

3. **The feelings of guilt should no longer be a problem with Christ as our Savior, our righteousness, and our intercessor.**

   Romans 8:33–35 Who will bring any charge against those whom God has chosen? It is God who justifies. Who is he that condemns? Christ Jesus, who died—more than that, who was raised to life—is at the right hand of God and is also interceding for us. Who shall separate us from the love of Christ? Shall trouble or hardship or persecution or famine or nakedness or danger or sword?

2 Corinthians 5:21 God made him who had no sin to be sin for us, so that in him we might become the righteousness of God.

Hebrews 7:25 Therefore he is able to save completely those who come to God through him, because he always lives to intercede for them.

Hebrews 9:24

4. **Even though we regret our sins, we must rely not on feelings but on the fact that, once forgiven, our sins have been thoroughly discarded.**

Micah 7:18–19 Who is a God like you, who pardons sin and forgives the transgression of the remnant of his inheritance? You do not stay angry forever but delight to show mercy. You will again have compassion on us; you will tread our sins underfoot and hurl all our iniquities into the depths of the sea.

Isaiah 43:25 I, even I, am he who blots out your transgressions, for my own sake, and remembers your sins no more.

Isaiah 38:17 In your love you kept me from the pit of destruction; you have put all my sins behind your back.

Psalm 103:12; Isaiah 1:18; Romans 4:7–8

5. **Replace guilt with proper thinking.**

Philippians 4:6–8 Do not be anxious about anything, but in everything, by prayer and petition, with thanksgiving, present your requests to God. And the peace of God, which transcends all understanding, will guard your hearts and your minds in Christ Jesus. Finally, brothers, whatever is true, whatever is noble, whatever is right, whatever is pure, whatever is lovely, whatever is admirable—if anything is excellent or praiseworthy—think about such things.

Biblical Illustration—David (2 Samuel 11; Psalm 51)

Health/Illness

See also Suffering, Natural Disasters, Fear, Trust, Special Needs

1. Health problems can be expected in this life.

Psalm 103:15–16 As for man, his days are like grass, he flourishes like a flower of the field; the wind blows over it and it is gone, and its place remembers it no more.

2 Corinthians 5:4 For while we are in this tent, we groan and are burdened, because we do not wish to be unclothed but to be clothed with our heavenly dwelling, so that what is mortal may be swallowed up by life.

2. God's presence in all trying situations is guaranteed. We are not alone.

Deuteronomy 31:6 Be strong and courageous. Do not be afraid or terrified because of them, for the LORD your God goes with you; he will never leave you nor forsake you.

Isaiah 43:1–2 But now, this is what the LORD says—he who created you, O Jacob, he who formed you, O Israel: "Fear not, for I have redeemed you; I have summoned you by name; you are mine. When you pass through the waters, I will be with you; and when you pass through the rivers, they will not sweep over you. When you walk through the fire, you will not be burned; the flames will not set you ablaze."

Isaiah 41:10, 13

3. Our all-powerful God gives strength.

Psalm 73:26 My flesh and my heart may fail, but God is the strength of my heart and my portion forever.

Psalm 91:4 He will cover you with his feathers, and under his wings you will find refuge; his faithfulness will be your shield and rampart.

2 Corinthians 4:7–9 But we have this treasure in jars of clay to show that this all-surpassing power is from God and not from us. We are hard pressed on every side, but not crushed; perplexed, but not in despair; persecuted, but not abandoned; struck down, but not destroyed.

2 Corinthians 4:16 Therefore we do not lose heart. Though outwardly we are wasting away, yet inwardly we are being renewed day by day.

2 Samuel 22:33; Psalm 31:24; Philippians 4:13

4. Health advice from Proverbs.

Proverbs 3:7–8 Do not be wise in your own eyes; fear the LORD and shun evil. This will bring health to your body and nourishment to your bones.

Proverbs 14:30 A heart at peace gives life to the body, but envy rots the bones.

Proverbs 18:14 A man's spirit sustains him in sickness, but a crushed spirit who can bear?

Proverbs 17:22

5. Whatever the final outcome of our health problems is, God will be glorified.

2 Corinthians 12:9–10 But he said to me, "My grace is sufficient for you, for my power is made perfect in weakness." Therefore I will boast all the more gladly about my weaknesses, so that Christ's power may rest on me. That is why, for Christ's sake, I delight in weaknesses, in insults, in hardships, in persecutions, in difficulties. For when I am weak, then I am strong.

1 Peter 1:6–7 In this you greatly rejoice, though now for a little while you may have had to suffer grief in all kinds of trials. These have come so that your faith—of greater worth than gold, which perishes even though refined by fire—may be proved genuine and may result in praise, glory and honor when Jesus Christ is revealed.

6. **God can and does heal, in his time, according to his will. God is the one who does the healing.**

   Psalm 30:2–3 O LORD my God, I called to you for help and you healed me. O LORD, you brought me up from the grave; you spared me from going down into the pit.

   James 5:14–16 Is any one of you sick? He should call the elders of the church to pray over him and anoint him with oil in the name of the Lord. And the prayer offered in faith will make the sick person well; the Lord will raise him up. If he has sinned, he will be forgiven. Therefore confess your sins to each other and pray for each other so that you may be healed. The prayer of a righteous man is powerful and effective.

   2 Kings 20:1–11; Psalm 103:2–5

7. **Health problems can help us grow as Christians.**

   James 1:2–4 Consider it pure joy, my brothers, whenever you face trials of many kinds, because you know that the testing of your faith develops perseverance. Perseverance must finish its work so that you may be mature and complete, not lacking anything.

   Psalm 119:71 It was good for me to be afflicted so that I might learn your decrees.

   Job 23:8–10

8. **Ultimately, heaven awaits us with its freedom from pain and illness.**

   Revelation 21:4 He will wipe every tear from their eyes. There will be no more death or mourning or crying or pain, for the old order of things has passed away.

   Philippians 3:20–21 But our citizenship is in heaven. And we eagerly await a Savior from there, the Lord Jesus Christ, who, by the power that enables him to bring everything under his control, will transform our lowly bodies so that they will be like his glorious body.

   Romans 8:18–19, 22–23

Heroes

1. Remember, it is the inside of people, not the outside, that should be admired.

1 Samuel 16:7 But the LORD said to Samuel, "Do not consider his appearance or his height, for I have rejected him. The LORD does not look at the things man looks at. Man looks at the outward appearance, but the LORD looks at the heart."

Proverbs 31:30 Charm is deceptive, and beauty is fleeting; but a woman who fears the LORD is to be praised.

2. Proud and boastful people do not make good heroes.

Jeremiah 9:23–24 This is what the LORD says: "Let not the wise man boast of his wisdom or the strong man boast of his strength or the rich man boast of his riches, but let him who boasts boast about this: that he understands and knows me, that I am the LORD, who exercises kindness, justice and righteousness on earth, for in these I delight," declares the LORD.

Isaiah 3:16 The LORD says, "The women of Zion are haughty, walking along with outstretched necks, flirting with their eyes, tripping along with mincing steps, with ornaments jingling on their ankles."

1 Peter 5:5

3. Admiration of heroes must not become idolatry.

Exodus 20:3–4 You shall have no other gods before me. You shall not make for yourself an idol in the form of anything in heaven above or on the earth beneath or in the waters below.

1 John 5:21 Dear children, keep yourselves from idols.

4. We must choose our heroes wisely.

Proverbs 2:11–15 Discretion will protect you, and understanding will guard you. Wisdom will save you from the ways of wicked men, from men whose words are perverse, who leave the straight paths to walk in dark ways, who delight in doing wrong and rejoice in the perverseness of evil, whose paths are crooked and who are devious in their ways.

Psalm 1:1

5. The ungodly are quickly gone and must not be looked up to or imitated.

Psalm 1:4–6 Not so the wicked! They are like chaff that the wind blows away. Therefore the wicked will not stand in the judgment, nor sinners in the assembly of the righteous. For the LORD watches over the way of the righteous, but the way of the wicked will perish.

Ephesians 5:3–5, 7 But among you there must not be even a hint of sexual immorality, or of any kind of impurity, or of greed, because these are improper for God's holy people. Nor should there be obscenity, foolish talk or coarse joking, which are out of place, but rather thanksgiving. For of this you can be sure: No immoral, impure or greedy person—such a man is an idolater—has any inheritance in the kingdom of Christ and of God. . . . Therefore do not be partners with them.

6. Jesus Christ is the greatest hero to admire, our best example to follow.

1 Peter 2:21 To this you were called, because Christ suffered for you, leaving you an example, that you should follow in his steps.

Philippians 2:5–7 Your attitude should be the same as that of Christ Jesus: Who, being in very nature God, did not consider equality with God something to be grasped, but made himself nothing, taking the very nature of a servant, being made in human likeness.

Biblical Illustrations—Men and women of Hebrews 11

Homosexuality

See also Choices, Forgiveness, Temptation

1. **Homosexuality in action or fantasy is sinful and sexually impure.**

   Romans 1:24–27 Therefore God gave them over in the sinful desires of their hearts to sexual impurity for the degrading of their bodies with one another. They exchanged the truth of God for a lie, and worshiped and served created things rather than the Creator— who is forever praised. Amen. Because of this, God gave them over to shameful lusts. Even their women exchanged natural relations for unnatural ones. In the same way the men also abandoned natural relations with women and were inflamed with lust for one another. Men committed indecent acts with other men, and received in themselves the due penalty for their perversion.

   Leviticus 20:13 If a man lies with a man as one lies with a woman, both of them have done what is detestable.

   Leviticus 18:22; Romans 8:5–8; Galatians 5:19–21; Jude 1:7

2. **As with any sexual sin, homosexuality does not satisfy the cravings of the human heart (love, joy, peace, contentment, wellness of body and soul)—only God does.**

   Jeremiah 2:13 My people have committed two sins: They have forsaken me, the spring of living water, and have dug their own cisterns, broken cisterns that cannot hold water.

   Isaiah 55:1–2 Come, all you who are thirsty, come to the waters; and you who have no money, come, buy and eat! Come, buy wine and milk without money and without cost. Why spend money on what is not bread, and your labor on what does not satisfy? Listen,

listen to me, and eat what is good, and your soul will delight in the richest of fare.

John 10:10

3. **The Christian must recognize that his or her body is a temple of the Holy Spirit and that he or she must flee from immorality.**

1 Corinthians 6:18–20 Flee from sexual immorality. All other sins a man commits are outside his body, but he who sins sexually sins against his own body. Do you not know that your body is a temple of the Holy Spirit, who is in you, whom you have received from God? You are not your own; you were bought at a price. Therefore honor God with your body.

Ephesians 5:11–12 Have nothing to do with the fruitless deeds of darkness, but rather expose them. For it is shameful even to mention what the disobedient do in secret.

4. **As with any sin, complete forgiveness is available.**

1 Corinthians 6:9–11 Do you not know that the wicked will not inherit the kingdom of God? Do not be deceived: Neither the sexually immoral nor idolaters nor adulterers nor male prostitutes nor homosexual offenders nor thieves nor the greedy nor drunkards nor slanderers nor swindlers will inherit the kingdom of God. And that is what some of you were. But you were washed, you were sanctified, you were justified in the name of the Lord Jesus Christ and by the Spirit of our God.

Micah 7:18–19 Who is a God like you, who pardons sin and forgives the transgression of the remnant of his inheritance? You do not stay angry forever but delight to show mercy. You will again have compassion on us; you will tread our sins underfoot and hurl all our iniquities into the depths of the sea.

Isaiah 43:25; 1 John 1:9

5. **With God's help, the potential for the homosexual to change is very real.**

2 Corinthians 5:17 Therefore, if anyone is in Christ, he is a new creation; the old has gone, the new has come!

John 8:36 So if the Son sets you free, you will be free indeed.

1 Corinthians 10:13 No temptation has seized you except what is common to man. And God is faithful; he will not let you be tempted beyond what you can bear. But when you are tempted, he will also provide a way out so that you can stand up under it.

Galatians 5:16 So I say, live by the Spirit, and you will not gratify the desires of the sinful nature.

Romans 7:23–25

6. Moral choices must be made.

Psalm 141:4 Let not my heart be drawn to what is evil, to take part in wicked deeds with men who are evildoers; let me not eat of their delicacies.

Romans 6:6, 11–14, 19 For we know that our old self was crucified with him so that the body of sin might be done away with, that we should no longer be slaves to sin. . . . In the same way, count yourselves dead to sin but alive to God in Christ Jesus. Therefore do not let sin reign in your mortal body so that you obey its evil desires. Do not offer the parts of your body to sin, as instruments of wickedness, but rather offer yourselves to God, as those who have been brought from death to life; and offer the parts of your body to him as instruments of righteousness. For sin shall not be your master, because you are not under law, but under grace. . . . I put this in human terms because you are weak in your natural selves. Just as you used to offer the parts of your body in slavery to impurity and to ever-increasing wickedness, so now offer them in slavery to righteousness leading to holiness.

[Note the "know," "count," "offer" sequence for action steps.]

2 Timothy 2:22 Flee the evil desires of youth, and pursue righteousness, faith, love and peace, along with those who call on the Lord out of a pure heart.

Ephesians 4:17–24; 1 Thessalonians 4:3–7

7. Use wisdom in avoiding evil situations.

Proverbs 1:10 My son, if sinners entice you, do not give in to them.

Proverbs 2:11–15 Discretion will protect you, and understanding will guard you. Wisdom will save you from the ways of wicked men, from men whose words are perverse, who leave the straight paths to walk in dark ways, who delight in doing wrong and rejoice in the perverseness of evil, whose paths are crooked and who are devious in their ways.

Proverbs 4:25–27 Let your eyes look straight ahead, fix your gaze directly before you. Make level paths for your feet and take only ways that are firm. Do not swerve to the right or the left; keep your foot from evil.

Proverbs 4:14–16

Biblical Illustration—Genesis 19:1–13

Incest

See also Abuse, Sexual Purity

1. **Sexual intimacy between family members, including adults and children, brothers and sisters, or others in the family, is clearly forbidden.**

   Leviticus 18:8–9 Do not have sexual relations with your father's wife; that would dishonor your father. Do not have sexual relations with your sister, either your father's daughter or your mother's daughter, whether she was born in the same home or elsewhere.

   1 Corinthians 5:1–2 It is actually reported that there is sexual immorality among you, and of a kind that does not occur even among pagans: A man has his father's wife. And you are proud! Shouldn't you rather have been filled with grief and have put out of your fellowship the man who did this?

   Leviticus 18:29–30; Galatians 5:19

2. **God sees hidden sin.**

   Luke 8:17 For there is nothing hidden that will not be disclosed, and nothing concealed that will not be known or brought out into the open.

   Psalm 139:1–5 O Lord, you have searched me and you know me. You know when I sit and when I rise; you perceive my thoughts from afar. You discern my going out and my lying down; you are familiar with all my ways. Before a word is on my tongue you know it completely, O Lord. You hem me in—behind and before; you have laid your hand upon me.

   Matthew 10:26

3. Steps need to be taken to end the sinful situation.

Matthew 18:15–17 If your brother sins against you, go and show him his fault, just between the two of you. If he listens to you, you have won your brother over. But if he will not listen, take one or two others along, so that "every matter may be established by the testimony of two or three witnesses." If he refuses to listen to them, tell it to the church; and if he refuses to listen even to the church, treat him as you would a pagan or a tax collector.

Galatians 6:1–2 Brothers, if someone is caught in a sin, you who are spiritual should restore him gently. But watch yourself, or you also may be tempted. Carry each other's burdens, and in this way you will fulfill the law of Christ.

Ephesians 4:17–19 So I tell you this, and insist on it in the Lord, that you must no longer live as the Gentiles do, in the futility of their thinking. They are darkened in their understanding and separated from the life of God because of the ignorance that is in them due to the hardening of their hearts. Having lost all sensitivity, they have given themselves over to sensuality so as to indulge in every kind of impurity, with a continual lust for more.

Proverbs 8:12–13

Biblical Illustrations—Lot (Genesis 19:30–38); 1 Corinthians 5

Note: It would be beneficial to have the counselee see a physician, pastor, or trained biblical counselor.

Integrity

See also Lying, Stealing

1. **Integrity is standing for what is right no matter what.**

   Psalm 15:1–4 LORD, who may dwell in your sanctuary? Who may live on your holy hill? He whose walk is blameless and who does what is righteous, who speaks the truth from his heart and has no slander on his tongue, who does his neighbor no wrong and casts no slur on his fellowman, who despises a vile man but honors those who fear the LORD, who keeps his oath even when it hurts.

   Micah 6:8 He has showed you, O man, what is good. And what does the LORD require of you? To act justly and to love mercy and to walk humbly with your God.

   Matthew 5:8

2. **Integrity put into practice brings blessing.**

   Proverbs 2:7–10 He holds victory in store for the upright, he is a shield to those whose walk is blameless, for he guards the course of the just and protects the way of his faithful ones. Then you will understand what is right and just and fair—every good path. For wisdom will enter your heart, and knowledge will be pleasant to your soul.

   Proverbs 10:9 The man of integrity walks securely, but he who takes crooked paths will be found out.

   Psalm 25:21 May integrity and uprightness protect me, because my hope is in you.

   Psalm 37:18; 119:1

3. Integrity put into practice can bring persecution.

Proverbs 29:10 Bloodthirsty men hate a man of integrity and seek to kill the upright.

Amos 5:10 You hate the one who reproves in court and despise him who tells the truth.

1 Peter 3:13–15 Who is going to harm you if you are eager to do good? But even if you should suffer for what is right, you are blessed. "Do not fear what they fear; do not be frightened." But in your hearts set apart Christ as Lord. Always be prepared to give an answer to everyone who asks you to give the reason for the hope that you have. But do this with gentleness and respect.

Matthew 5:10–11

4. Keeping our integrity takes commitment to doing what is right.

Proverbs 28:6 Better a poor man whose walk is blameless than a rich man whose ways are perverse.

Titus 2:6–8 Similarly, encourage the young men to be self-controlled. In everything set them an example by doing what is good. In your teaching show integrity, seriousness and soundness of speech that cannot be condemned, so that those who oppose you may be ashamed because they have nothing bad to say about us.

Philippians 1:9–11 And this is my prayer: that your love may abound more and more in knowledge and depth of insight, so that you may be able to discern what is best and may be pure and blameless until the day of Christ, filled with the fruit of righteousness that comes through Jesus Christ—to the glory and praise of God.

Jealousy/Envy

See also Bitterness, Contentment, Complaining

1. **Jealousy is sinful, is displeasing to God, and leads to the sin of wanting what someone else has (envying or coveting).**

   James 3:14–16 But if you harbor bitter envy and selfish ambition in your hearts, do not boast about it or deny the truth. Such "wisdom" does not come down from heaven but is earthly, unspiritual, of the devil. For where you have envy and selfish ambition, there you find disorder and every evil practice.

   1 Corinthians 3:3 You are still worldly. For since there is jealousy and quarreling among you, are you not worldly? Are you not acting like mere men?

   Galatians 5:26 Let us not become conceited, provoking and envying each other.

   Exodus 20:17 You shall not covet your neighbor's house. You shall not covet your neighbor's wife, or his manservant or maidservant, his ox or donkey, or anything that belongs to your neighbor.

2. **Jealousy must be confessed and removed from your life.**

   1 Peter 2:1 Therefore, rid yourselves of all malice and all deceit, hypocrisy, envy, and slander of every kind.

   1 John 1:8–10

3. **Loving others and placing them first is key to overcoming this sin.**

   John 13:34 A new command I give you: Love one another. As I have loved you, so you must love one another.

1 Corinthians 13:4 Love is patient, love is kind. It does not envy, it does not boast, it is not proud.

Romans 13:9–10 The commandments, "Do not commit adultery," "Do not murder," "Do not steal," "Do not covet," and whatever other commandment there may be, are summed up in this one rule: "Love your neighbor as yourself." Love does no harm to its neighbor. Therefore love is the fulfillment of the law.

Philippians 2:3–4; 1 Peter 1:22

4. God is all we need, and he will satisfy us.

Proverbs 23:17 Do not let your heart envy sinners, but always be zealous for the fear of the LORD.

Hebrews 13:5 Keep your lives free from the love of money and be content with what you have, because God has said, "Never will I leave you; never will I forsake you."

Philippians 4:11–13, 19 I am not saying this because I am in need, for I have learned to be content whatever the circumstances. I know what it is to be in need, and I know what it is to have plenty. I have learned the secret of being content in any and every situation, whether well fed or hungry, whether living in plenty or in want. I can do everything through him who gives me strength. . . . And my God will meet all your needs according to his glorious riches in Christ Jesus.

Psalm 37:1, 7; 73:25–26

Biblical Illustrations—Ahab and Jezebel (1 Kings 21); Asaph (Psalm 73); David (Psalm 37)

Laziness

See also Work Ethic, Time Management

1. Laziness is an excuse.

Proverbs 26:13–16 The sluggard says, "There is a lion in the road, a fierce lion roaming the streets!" As a door turns on its hinges, so a sluggard turns on his bed. The sluggard buries his hand in the dish; he is too lazy to bring it back to his mouth. The sluggard is wiser in his own eyes than seven men who answer discreetly.

Proverbs 22:13

2. Laziness can result in poverty.

Proverbs 24:30–34 I went past the field of the sluggard, past the vineyard of the man who lacks judgment; thorns had come up everywhere, the ground was covered with weeds, and the stone wall was in ruins. I applied my heart to what I observed and learned a lesson from what I saw: A little sleep, a little slumber, a little folding of the hands to rest—and poverty will come on you like a bandit and scarcity like an armed man.

Proverbs 19:15 Laziness brings on deep sleep, and the shiftless man goes hungry.

Ecclesiastes 10:18 If a man is lazy, the rafters sag; if his hands are idle, the house leaks.

Proverbs 6:6–11; 13:4; 20:4

3. Hard work was commanded by God even before the fall; a life of ease is not in his plan.

Genesis 2:15 The LORD God took the man and put him in the Garden of Eden to work it and take care of it.

Ecclesiastes 9:10 Whatever your hand finds to do, do it with all your might, for in the grave, where you are going, there is neither working nor planning nor knowledge nor wisdom.

2 Thessalonians 3:10–12 For even when we were with you, we gave you this rule: "If a man will not work, he shall not eat." We hear that some among you are idle. They are not busy; they are busybodies. Such people we command and urge in the Lord Jesus Christ to settle down and earn the bread they eat.

Hebrews 6:12

4. Time is a gift from God to be used wisely.

Psalm 39:4 Show me, O LORD, my life's end and the number of my days; let me know how fleeting is my life.

Job 16:22 Only a few years will pass before I go on the journey of no return.

Ephesians 5:15–17 Be very careful, then, how you live—not as unwise but as wise, making the most of every opportunity, because the days are evil. Therefore do not be foolish, but understand what the Lord's will is.

Psalm 90:12; Proverbs 10:5

5. Self-discipline is a quality of life that gets things accomplished.

1 Corinthians 9:24–27 Do you not know that in a race all the runners run, but only one gets the prize? Run in such a way as to get the prize. Everyone who competes in the games goes into strict training. They do it to get a crown that will not last; but we do it to get a crown that will last forever. Therefore I do not run like a man running aimlessly; I do not fight like a man beating the air. No, I beat my body and make it my slave so that after I have preached to others, I myself will not be disqualified for the prize.

6. God is our standard, our judge, in every matter—work (or lack of it) included.

Ecclesiastes 12:13–14 Now all has been heard; here is the conclusion of the matter: Fear God and keep his commandments, for this is the whole duty of man. For God will bring every deed into judgment, including every hidden thing, whether it is good or evil.

Biblical Illustrations—Israel not rebuilding the temple (Haggai 1); Paul (2 Thessalonians 3:6–9)

Loneliness

See also Fear, Singleness

1. The reality of loneliness can be devastating.

Job 19:13–14 He has alienated my brothers from me; my acquaintances are completely estranged from me. My kinsmen have gone away; my friends have forgotten me.

Psalm 38:9–11 All my longings lie open before you, O Lord; my sighing is not hidden from you. My heart pounds, my strength fails me; even the light has gone from my eyes. My friends and companions avoid me because of my wounds; my neighbors stay far away.

Psalm 102:7–11 I lie awake; I have become like a bird alone on a roof. All day long my enemies taunt me; those who rail against me use my name as a curse. For I eat ashes as my food and mingle my drink with tears because of your great wrath, for you have taken me up and thrown me aside. My days are like the evening shadow; I wither away like grass.

2. Sometimes we feel separated from God, as if he has left us.

Job 23:8–9 But if I go to the east, he is not there; if I go to the west, I do not find him. When he is at work in the north, I do not see him; when he turns to the south, I catch no glimpse of him.

Psalm 13:1 How long, O LORD? Will you forget me forever? How long will you hide your face from me?

3. God is always there and does respond with comfort and help.

Psalm 25:16 Turn to me and be gracious to me, for I am lonely and afflicted.

Psalm 73:25–26 Whom have I in heaven but you? And earth has nothing I desire besides you. My flesh and my heart may fail, but God is the strength of my heart and my portion forever.

Psalm 13:5–6; 62:1–2; 142:1–4

4. God will provide for our emotional and spiritual needs when we feel alone.

Psalm 68:5–6 A father to the fatherless, a defender of widows, is God in his holy dwelling. God sets the lonely in families, he leads forth the prisoners with singing; but the rebellious live in a sunscorched land.

Joshua 1:9 Have I not commanded you? Be strong and courageous. Do not be terrified; do not be discouraged, for the LORD your God will be with you wherever you go.

Romans 8:38–39

5. Paul's solution to loneliness.

2 Timothy 4:16–18 At my first defense, no one came to my support, but everyone deserted me. May it not be held against them. But the Lord stood at my side and gave me strength, so that through me the message might be fully proclaimed and all the Gentiles might hear it. And I was delivered from the lion's mouth. The Lord will rescue me from every evil attack and will bring me safely to his heavenly kingdom. To him be glory for ever and ever. Amen.

6. God provided for Elijah's needs when he felt alone.

1 Kings 19:10 He replied, "I have been very zealous for the LORD God Almighty. The Israelites have rejected your covenant, broken down your altars, and put your prophets to death with the sword. I am the only one left, and now they are trying to kill me too."

I Kings 19:1–18

Biblical Illustrations—Adam in the garden (Genesis 2:18, 21–23); Jesus on the cross (Matthew 27:46)

Lust

See also Thought Life, Masturbation, Pornography, Temptation

1. **Lust begins in the mind and is a desire for that which God has forbidden.**

    Exodus 20:17 You shall not covet your neighbor's house. You shall not covet your neighbor's wife, or his manservant or maidservant, his ox or donkey, or anything that belongs to your neighbor.

    Matthew 5:28 But I tell you that anyone who looks at a woman lustfully has already committed adultery with her in his heart.

    1 Peter 2:11 Dear friends, I urge you, as aliens and strangers in the world, to abstain from sinful desires, which war against your soul.

2. **Lust is serious because it begins a downward spiral of evil, with serious consequences.**

    Joshua 7:20–21 Achan replied, "It is true! I have sinned against the LORD, the God of Israel. This is what I have done: When I saw in the plunder a beautiful robe from Babylonia, two hundred shekels of silver and a wedge of gold weighing fifty shekels, I coveted them and took them. They are hidden in the ground inside my tent, with the silver underneath."

    James 1:14–15 But each one is tempted when, by his own evil desire, he is dragged away and enticed. Then, after desire has conceived, it gives birth to sin; and sin, when it is full-grown, gives birth to death.

3. **Each young person must guard against individual areas of temptation.**

    Proverbs 4:23 Above all else, guard your heart, for it is the wellspring of life.

Job 31:1 I made a covenant with my eyes not to look lustfully at a girl.

1 Thessalonians 4:3–4 It is God's will that you should be sanctified: that you should avoid sexual immorality; that each of you should learn to control his own body in a way that is holy and honorable.

4. **With God's help in making good choices, it is possible to put aside lustful thoughts.**

Titus 2:11–12 For the grace of God that brings salvation has appeared to all men. It teaches us to say "No" to ungodliness and worldly passions, and to live self-controlled, upright and godly lives in this present age.

1 Corinthians 10:13 No temptation has seized you except what is common to man. And God is faithful; he will not let you be tempted beyond what you can bear. But when you are tempted, he will also provide a way out so that you can stand up under it.

Biblical Illustrations—Lot, who moved closer and closer to sin (Genesis 13; 18–19); Achan (Joshua 7)

Lying/Truthfulness

See also Words That Hurt, Stealing

1. Lying is forbidden by God; it is always wrong.

Leviticus 19:11–12 Do not steal. Do not lie. Do not deceive one another. Do not swear falsely by my name and so profane the name of your God. I am the LORD.

Psalm 34:13 Keep your tongue from evil and your lips from speaking lies.

Colossians 3:9 Do not lie to each other, since you have taken off your old self with its practices.

Exodus 20:16; 23:1

2. Lying is detestable to God.

Proverbs 6:16–19 There are six things the LORD hates, seven that are detestable to him: haughty eyes, a lying tongue, hands that shed innocent blood, a heart that devises wicked schemes, feet that are quick to rush into evil, a false witness who pours out lies and a man who stirs up dissension among brothers.

Proverbs 12:22 The LORD detests lying lips, but he delights in men who are truthful.

Psalm 5:6

3. Lying is a sin that is a struggle from birth.

Psalm 58:3 Even from birth the wicked go astray; from the womb they are wayward and speak lies.

Psalm 51:5 Surely I was sinful at birth, sinful from the time my mother conceived me.

Matthew 15:19; Romans 3:13

4. Telling the complete truth is the only choice for the believer.

Ephesians 4:25 Therefore each of you must put off falsehood and speak truthfully to his neighbor, for we are all members of one body.

Psalm 15:1–2 LORD, who may dwell in your sanctuary? Who may live on your holy hill? He whose walk is blameless and who does what is righteous, who speaks the truth from his heart.

James 1:26 If anyone considers himself religious and yet does not keep a tight rein on his tongue, he deceives himself and his religion is worthless.

5. Not telling the truth has consequences.

Psalm 63:11 The mouths of liars will be silenced.

Psalm 24:3–4 Who may ascend the hill of the LORD? Who may stand in his holy place? He who has clean hands and a pure heart, who does not lift up his soul to an idol or swear by what is false.

Proverbs 12:13 An evil man is trapped by his sinful talk, but a righteous man escapes trouble.

Proverbs 19:5 A false witness will not go unpunished, and he who pours out lies will not go free.

Psalm 12:2–4; 17:1; 101:7

Biblical Illustrations—Abraham (Genesis 12:1–20); Jacob (Genesis 27)

Manipulation

See also Speech

1. **Arranging situations or manipulating people for one's personal advancement or benefit is wrong in God's sight.**

    Psalm 101:7 No one who practices deceit will dwell in my house; no one who speaks falsely will stand in my presence.

    Proverbs 12:2 A good man obtains favor from the LORD, but the LORD condemns a crafty man.

    Proverbs 6:16–18 There are six things the LORD hates, seven that are detestable to him: haughty eyes, a lying tongue, hands that shed innocent blood, a heart that devises wicked schemes, feet that are quick to rush into evil.

    Proverbs 24:28

2. **Manipulation leads to God's judgment.**

    Job 32:21–22 I will show partiality to no one, nor will I flatter any man; for if I were skilled in flattery, my Maker would soon take me away.

    Psalm 7:15–16 He who digs a hole and scoops it out falls into the pit he has made. The trouble he causes recoils on himself; his violence comes down on his own head.

    Proverbs 10:9 The man of integrity walks securely, but he who takes crooked paths will be found out.

    Psalm 32:2

3. **Manipulation often begins with the wrong use of one's speech.**

Proverbs 16:30 He who winks with his eye is plotting perversity; he who purses his lips is bent on evil.

Psalm 50:19 You use your mouth for evil and harness your tongue to deceit.

Psalm 34:13; 52:4

4. **Watch out for those who use flattery for manipulation.**

Romans 16:18 For such people are not serving our Lord Christ, but their own appetites. By smooth talk and flattery they deceive the minds of naive people.

Proverbs 26:28 A lying tongue hates those it hurts, and a flattering mouth works ruin.

Psalm 12:2–4 Everyone lies to his neighbor; their flattering lips speak with deception. May the LORD cut off all flattering lips and every boastful tongue that says, "We will triumph with our tongues; we own our lips—who is our master?"

1 Thessalonians 2:5

5. **Stay away from those who devise schemes—don't get caught up with them.**

Proverbs 14:7 Stay away from a foolish man, for you will not find knowledge on his lips.

Psalm 56:5–6 All day long they twist my words; they are always plotting to harm me. They conspire, they lurk, they watch my steps, eager to take my life.

Psalm 64:5–6 They encourage each other in evil plans, they talk about hiding their snares; they say, "Who will see them?" They plot injustice and say, "We have devised a perfect plan!" Surely the mind and heart of man are cunning.

Proverbs 27:6; Ephesians 5:6

Biblical Illustration—Laban (Genesis 24:28–31)

Marriage

See also Sexual Purity

1. **From the beginning, marriage was a part of God's design for us. One man, one woman.**

   Genesis 2:22–25 Then the LORD God made a woman from the rib he had taken out of the man, and he brought her to the man. The man said, "This is now bone of my bones and flesh of my flesh; she shall be called 'woman,' for she was taken out of man." For this reason a man will leave his father and mother and be united to his wife, and they will become one flesh. The man and his wife were both naked, and they felt no shame.

2. **Marriage is a permanent covenant for life. Living together without that marriage covenant is immoral.**

   Malachi 2:14 You ask, "Why?" It is because the LORD is acting as the witness between you and the wife of your youth, because you have broken faith with her, though she is your partner, the wife of your marriage covenant.

   Hebrews 13:4 Marriage should be honored by all, and the marriage bed kept pure, for God will judge the adulterer and all the sexually immoral.

   1 Corinthians 7:2 But since there is so much immorality, each man should have his own wife, and each woman her own husband.

   Proverbs 2:17; Mark 10:7–9

3. Believers should marry only other believers.

2 Corinthians 6:14 Do not be yoked together with unbelievers. For what do righteousness and wickedness have in common? Or what fellowship can light have with darkness?

Roles in Marriage

1. Husband—loving leader.

Ephesians 5:23–28 For the husband is the head of the wife as Christ is the head of the church, his body, of which he is the Savior. Now as the church submits to Christ, so also wives should submit to their husbands in everything. Husbands, love your wives, just as Christ loved the church and gave himself up for her to make her holy, cleansing her by the washing with water through the word, and to present her to himself as a radiant church, without stain or wrinkle or any other blemish, but holy and blameless. In this same way, husbands ought to love their wives as their own bodies. He who loves his wife loves himself.

1 Peter 3:7 Husbands, in the same way be considerate as you live with your wives, and treat them with respect as the weaker partner and as heirs with you of the gracious gift of life, so that nothing will hinder your prayers.

Colossians 3:19

2. Wife—respectful completer.

Genesis 2:18, 20–22 The Lord God said, "It is not good for the man to be alone. I will make a helper suitable for him." . . . So the man gave names to all the livestock, the birds of the air and all the beasts of the field. But for Adam no suitable helper was found. So the Lord God caused the man to fall into a deep sleep; and while he was sleeping, he took one of the man's ribs and closed up the place with flesh. Then the Lord God made a woman from the rib he had taken out of the man, and he brought her to the man.

Ephesians 5:22–23 Wives, submit to your husbands as to the Lord. For the husband is the head of the wife as Christ is the head of the church, his body, of which he is the Savior.

137

Proverbs 14:1 The wise woman builds her house, but with her own hands the foolish one tears hers down.

Proverbs 19:13–14 A foolish son is his father's ruin, and a quarrelsome wife is like a constant dripping. Houses and wealth are inherited from parents, but a prudent wife is from the LORD.

Proverbs 12:4; Colossians 3:18; 1 Peter 3:1

Masturbation

See also Lust, Pornography, Temptation, Sexual Purity

1. While there is no direct mention of this in Scripture, certain principles do apply.

Selfishness

Romans 13:14 Rather, clothe yourselves with the Lord Jesus Christ, and do not think about how to gratify the desires of the sinful nature.

Colossians 3:5 Put to death, therefore, whatever belongs to your earthly nature: sexual immorality, impurity, lust, evil desires and greed, which is idolatry.

James 1:14–15 But each one is tempted when, by his own evil desire, he is dragged away and enticed. Then, after desire has conceived, it gives birth to sin; and sin, when it is full-grown, gives birth to death.

Exodus 20:3–4

Mental Images

2 Corinthians 10:5 We demolish arguments and every pretension that sets itself up against the knowledge of God, and we take captive every thought to make it obedient to Christ.

Ephesians 5:3 But among you there must not be even a hint of sexual immorality, or of any kind of impurity, or of greed, because these are improper for God's holy people.

Matthew 5:28 But I tell you that anyone who looks at a woman lustfully has already committed adultery with her in his heart.

Heart Issues

Psalm 51:10 Create in me a pure heart, O God, and renew a steadfast spirit within me.

Mark 7:20–23 What comes out of a man is what makes him "unclean." For from within, out of men's hearts, come evil thoughts, sexual immorality, theft, murder, adultery, greed, malice, deceit, lewdness, envy, slander, arrogance and folly. All these evils come from inside and make a man "unclean."

Psalm 19:14; Jeremiah 17:9–10

2. Secret activity and isolation are to be avoided.

Ephesians 5:11–12 Have nothing to do with the fruitless deeds of darkness, but rather expose them. For it is shameful even to mention what the disobedient do in secret.

Ecclesiastes 12:13–14 Now all has been heard; here is the conclusion of the matter: Fear God and keep his commandments, for this is the whole duty of man. For God will bring every deed into judgment, including every hidden thing, whether it is good or evil.

Proverbs 28:13

3. God offers escape from sin and gives blessing.

2 Corinthians 7:1 Since we have these promises, dear friends, let us purify ourselves from everything that contaminates body and spirit, perfecting holiness out of reverence for God.

1 Corinthians 10:13 No temptation has seized you except what is common to man. And God is faithful; he will not let you be tempted beyond what you can bear. But when you are tempted, he will also provide a way out so that you can stand up under it.

Psalm 24:3–5

4. One reason that God designed marriage was to alleviate problems of lust. Save your body for the mate whom God will give you.

1 Corinthians 7:1–4 Now for the matters you wrote about: It is good for a man not to marry. But since there is so much immorality, each man should have his own wife, and each woman her own husband. The husband should fulfill his marital duty to his wife, and likewise the wife to her husband. The wife's body does not belong to her alone but also to her husband. In the same way, the husband's body does not belong to him alone but also to his wife.

Genesis 2:21–24

Materialism

See also Contentment, Jealousy, Money

1. Riches in heaven are better than riches on earth.

Matthew 6:19–21 Do not store up for yourselves treasures on earth, where moth and rust destroy, and where thieves break in and steal. But store up for yourselves treasures in heaven, where moth and rust do not destroy, and where thieves do not break in and steal. For where your treasure is, there your heart will be also.

1 Corinthians 3:11–15 For no one can lay any foundation other than the one already laid, which is Jesus Christ. If any man builds on this foundation using gold, silver, costly stones, wood, hay or straw, his work will be shown for what it is, because the Day will bring it to light. It will be revealed with fire, and the fire will test the quality of each man's work. If what he has built survives, he will receive his reward. If it is burned up, he will suffer loss; he himself will be saved, but only as one escaping through the flames.

1 Timothy 6:17–19

2. The desire for more possessions can lead to a trap of ruin.

1 Timothy 6:6–9 But godliness with contentment is great gain. For we brought nothing into the world, and we can take nothing out of it. But if we have food and clothing, we will be content with that. People who want to get rich fall into temptation and a trap and into many foolish and harmful desires that plunge men into ruin and destruction.

Psalm 73:2–3 But as for me, my feet had almost slipped; I had nearly lost my foothold. For I envied the arrogant when I saw the prosperity of the wicked.

Proverbs 11:28 Whoever trusts in his riches will fall, but the righteous will thrive like a green leaf.

Proverbs 28:25–26; James 5:1–3

3. Desire for riches can sidetrack individuals from their beliefs.

Matthew 6:24 No one can serve two masters. Either he will hate the one and love the other, or he will be devoted to the one and despise the other. You cannot serve both God and Money.

1 Timothy 6:10 For the love of money is a root of all kinds of evil. Some people, eager for money, have wandered from the faith and pierced themselves with many griefs.

Proverbs 30:8–9; 1 John 2:15

4. Security is not found in possessions.

Psalm 49:16–17 Do not be overawed when a man grows rich, when the splendor of his house increases; for he will take nothing with him when he dies, his splendor will not descend with him.

Isaiah 58:11 The LORD will guide you always; he will satisfy your needs in a sun-scorched land and will strengthen your frame. You will be like a well-watered garden, like a spring whose waters never fail.

Luke 12:15 Then he said to them, "Watch out! Be on your guard against all kinds of greed; a man's life does not consist in the abundance of his possessions."

1 Timothy 6:17 Command those who are rich in this present world not to be arrogant nor to put their hope in wealth, which is so uncertain, but to put their hope in God, who richly provides us with everything for our enjoyment.

Proverbs 23:4–5; 28:6; Hebrews 13:5

5. Solutions for avoiding materialism.

Colossians 3:1–3 Since, then, you have been raised with Christ, set your hearts on things above, where Christ is seated at the right hand of God. Set your minds on things above, not on earthly things. For you died, and your life is now hidden with Christ in God.

Philippians 4:11–13 I am not saying this because I am in need, for I have learned to be content whatever the circumstances. I know what it is to be in need, and I know what it is to have plenty. I have learned the secret of being content in any and every situation, whether well fed or hungry, whether living in plenty or in want. I can do everything through him who gives me strength.

Philippians 3:7–8

6. **Giving willingly to God's work or to those less fortunate is a blessing for those giving as well as for those receiving.**

   2 Corinthians 9:6–8 Remember this: Whoever sows sparingly will also reap sparingly, and whoever sows generously will also reap generously. Each man should give what he has decided in his heart to give, not reluctantly or under compulsion, for God loves a cheerful giver. And God is able to make all grace abound to you, so that in all things at all times, having all that you need, you will abound in every good work.

   1 Timothy 6:18–19 Command them to do good, to be rich in good deeds, and to be generous and willing to share. In this way they will lay up treasure for themselves as a firm foundation for the coming age, so that they may take hold of the life that is truly life.

   Proverbs 31:8–9 Speak up for those who cannot speak for themselves, for the rights of all who are destitute. Speak up and judge fairly; defend the rights of the poor and needy.

Biblical Illustrations—Achan (Joshua 7); Gehazi (2 Kings 5:20–27); Psalm 40

Money

See also Contentment, Jealousy, Materialism

Handling the Green Stuff—Some of the Basics

1. **Part of what we earn should be given back to God. Grace giving can include the tithing standard of the Old Testament.**

   Malachi 3:8 Will a man rob God? Yet you rob me. But you ask, "How do we rob you?" In tithes and offerings.

   Proverbs 3:9–10 Honor the LORD with your wealth, with the firstfruits of all your crops; then your barns will be filled to overflowing, and your vats will brim over with new wine.

   2 Corinthians 9:6–7 Remember this: Whoever sows sparingly will also reap sparingly, and whoever sows generously will also reap generously. Each man should give what he has decided in his heart to give, not reluctantly or under compulsion, for God loves a cheerful giver.

2. **Never be late in paying your bills, and do not borrow more than you can pay back.**

   Romans 13:8 Let no debt remain outstanding, except the continuing debt to love one another, for he who loves his fellowman has fulfilled the law.

3. **Work for what you get.**

   1 Thessalonians 4:11–12 Make it your ambition to lead a quiet life, to mind your own business and to work with your hands, just as we told you, so that your daily life may win the respect of outsiders and so that you will not be dependent on anybody.

145

2 Thessalonians 3:10 For even when we were with you, we gave you this rule: "If a man will not work, he shall not eat."

4. Be careful of taking on someone else's debt.

Proverbs 6:1–3 My son, if you have put up security for your neighbor, if you have struck hands in pledge for another, if you have been trapped by what you said, ensnared by the words of your mouth, then do this, my son, to free yourself, since you have fallen into your neighbor's hands: Go and humble yourself; press your plea with your neighbor!

Proverbs 11:15; 22:26

5. Recognize your responsibility for paying taxes.

Romans 13:1, 6–7 Everyone must submit himself to the governing authorities, for there is no authority except that which God has established. The authorities that exist have been established by God. . . . This is also why you pay taxes, for the authorities are God's servants, who give their full time to governing. Give everyone what you owe him: If you owe taxes, pay taxes; if revenue, then revenue; if respect, then respect; if honor, then honor.

Matthew 22:15–22

6. Planning for future needs (i.e., saving) is a wise course of action.

Proverbs 6:6–8 Go to the ant, you sluggard; consider its ways and be wise! It has no commander, no overseer or ruler, yet it stores its provisions in summer and gathers its food at harvest.

Proverbs 10:5 He who gathers crops in summer is a wise son, but he who sleeps during harvest is a disgraceful son.

7. Maintain a good reputation, financially and otherwise.

1 Timothy 3:7 He must also have a good reputation with outsiders, so that he will not fall into disgrace and into the devil's trap.

8. Asking for wisdom is important in every area of life, including financially.

James 1:5 If any of you lacks wisdom, he should ask God, who gives generously to all without finding fault, and it will be given to him.

Moving

(New Residence)

See also Fear, Loneliness, Trust, Worry

1. **God has promised to be with us in every situation—even moving to a new place.**

   Exodus 33:14 The LORD replied, "My Presence will go with you, and I will give you rest."

   Psalm 34:18 The LORD is close to the brokenhearted and saves those who are crushed in spirit.

   Hebrews 13:5 Be content with what you have, because God has said, "Never will I leave you; never will I forsake you."

   Deuteronomy 31:8; Psalm 73:23

2. **God will provide for all our needs in our new setting.**

   Deuteronomy 31:6 Be strong and courageous. Do not be afraid or terrified because of them, for the LORD your God goes with you; he will never leave you nor forsake you.

   Psalm 34:4 I sought the LORD, and he answered me; he delivered me from all my fears.

   Psalm 103:2, 4–5 Praise the LORD, O my soul, and forget not all his benefits . . . who redeems your life from the pit and crowns you with love and compassion, who satisfies your desires with good things so that your youth is renewed like the eagle's.

   Isaiah 41:10 So do not fear, for I am with you; do not be dismayed, for I am your God. I will strengthen you and help you; I will uphold you with my righteous right hand.

3. **Honor and respect for parents must be maintained, even though moving to a new location can be upsetting.**

   Exodus 20:12 Honor your father and your mother, so that you may live long in the land the LORD your God is giving you.

   Ephesians 6:1 Children, obey your parents in the Lord, for this is right.

   Psalm 84:11 For the LORD God is a sun and shield; the LORD bestows favor and honor; no good thing does he withhold from those whose walk is blameless.

Biblical Illustrations—Abraham, who moved far away to great blessing (Genesis 12); the Israelites, who moved out of Egypt to a new land of blessing (narratives of Exodus, Numbers, and Joshua)

Natural Disasters/Disease

See also Suffering, Fear, Health, Trust

1. **Because of Adam and Eve's sin in the Garden of Eden, every aspect of creation has been brought to a state of change and decay.**

   Genesis 3:17–18 To Adam he said, "Because you listened to your wife and ate from the tree about which I commanded you, 'You must not eat of it,' cursed is the ground because of you; through painful toil you will eat of it all the days of your life. It will produce thorns and thistles for you, and you will eat the plants of the field."

   Romans 8:20–22 For the creation was subjected to frustration, not by its own choice, but by the will of the one who subjected it, in hope that the creation itself will be liberated from its bondage to decay and brought into the glorious freedom of the children of God. We know that the whole creation has been groaning as in the pains of childbirth right up to the present time.

2. **Yet God has given us hope in his promise, as a part of his complete redemptive plan, to remove this curse of decay from all of creation.**

   Revelation 21:4–5 He will wipe every tear from their eyes. There will be no more death or mourning or crying or pain, for the old order of things has passed away. He who was seated on the throne said, "I am making everything new!" Then he said, "Write this down, for these words are trustworthy and true."

   Revelation 22:3 No longer will there be any curse. The throne of God and of the Lamb will be in the city, and his servants will serve him.

Romans 8:21 That the creation itself will be liberated from its bondage to decay and brought into the glorious freedom of the children of God.

Isaiah 25:8

3. God remains sovereign over all his creation.

Psalm 33:11 But the plans of the LORD stand firm forever, the purposes of his heart through all generations.

Jeremiah 10:12–13 But God made the earth by his power; he founded the world by his wisdom and stretched out the heavens by his understanding. When he thunders, the waters in the heavens roar; he makes clouds rise from the ends of the earth. He sends lightning with the rain and brings out the wind from his storehouses.

Job 9:5–10

4. Scripture shows that the blessings of heaven and eternity far outweigh the present frustrations of physical suffering.

2 Corinthians 4:16–18 Therefore we do not lose heart. Though outwardly we are wasting away, yet inwardly we are being renewed day by day. For our light and momentary troubles are achieving for us an eternal glory that far outweighs them all. So we fix our eyes not on what is seen, but on what is unseen. For what is seen is temporary, but what is unseen is eternal.

2 Corinthians 5:1–4 Now we know that if the earthly tent we live in is destroyed, we have a building from God, an eternal house in heaven, not built by human hands. Meanwhile we groan, longing to be clothed with our heavenly dwelling, because when we are clothed, we will not be found naked. For while we are in this tent, we groan and are burdened, because we do not wish to be unclothed but to be clothed with our heavenly dwelling, so that what is mortal may be swallowed up by life.

John 16:33

Biblical Illustration—Joel 1

Orphan

See also Adoption, Death, Loneliness

1. **Even if human parents are not able to be part of their child's life, our heavenly Father is actively involved.**

   Psalm 27:10 Though my father and mother forsake me, the LORD will receive me.

   2 Corinthians 6:18 "I will be a Father to you, and you will be my sons and daughters," says the Lord Almighty.

   Isaiah 49:15–16 Can a mother forget the baby at her breast and have no compassion on the child she has borne? Though she may forget, I will not forget you! See, I have engraved you on the palms of my hands; your walls are ever before me.

   Isaiah 66:13; Jeremiah 31:3

2. **God has a concern for those without parents and instructs others to defend and care for them.**

   Proverbs 23:10–11 Do not move an ancient boundary stone or encroach on the fields of the fatherless, for their Defender is strong; he will take up their case against you.

   Psalm 82:3–4 Defend the cause of the weak and fatherless; maintain the rights of the poor and oppressed. Rescue the weak and needy; deliver them from the hand of the wicked.

   Psalm 10:14, 17–18 But you, O God, do see trouble and grief; you consider it to take it in hand. The victim commits himself to you; you are the helper of the fatherless. . . . You hear, O LORD, the desire of the afflicted; you encourage them, and you listen to their cry, defending the fatherless and the oppressed, in order that man, who is of the earth, may terrify no more.

James 1:27 Religion that God our Father accepts as pure and faultless is this: to look after orphans and widows in their distress and to keep oneself from being polluted by the world.

Psalm 146:9; Jeremiah 22:3

3. A personal relationship with Jesus Christ is the ultimate family relationship.

1 John 3:1 How great is the love the Father has lavished on us, that we should be called children of God! And that is what we are! The reason the world does not know us is that it did not know him.

Ephesians 1:4–6 For he chose us in him before the creation of the world to be holy and blameless in his sight. In love he predestined us to be adopted as his sons through Jesus Christ, in accordance with his pleasure and will—to the praise of his glorious grace, which he has freely given us in the One he loves.

Parents

See also Authority

1. Most parents love their children and do their best to provide for their needs.

Matthew 7:9–11 Which of you, if his son asks for bread, will give him a stone? Or if he asks for a fish, will give him a snake? If you, then, though you are evil, know how to give good gifts to your children, how much more will your Father in heaven give good gifts to those who ask him!

2. Parents should impart godly wisdom; it is their responsibility.

Deuteronomy 6:6–7 These commandments that I give you today are to be upon your hearts. Impress them on your children. Talk about them when you sit at home and when you walk along the road, when you lie down and when you get up.

Psalm 78:5–7 He decreed statutes for Jacob and established the law in Israel, which he commanded our forefathers to teach their children, so the next generation would know them, even the children yet to be born, and they in turn would tell their children. Then they would put their trust in God and would not forget his deeds but would keep his commands.

1 Thessalonians 2:11–12 For you know that we dealt with each of you as a father deals with his own children, encouraging, comforting and urging you to live lives worthy of God, who calls you into his kingdom and glory.

Joshua 4:21–22; Psalm 44:1; Proverbs 4:3–4

3. Pay attention to parental wisdom and instruction.

Proverbs 1:8 Listen, my son, to your father's instruction and do not forsake your mother's teaching.

Proverbs 13:1 A wise son heeds his father's instruction, but a mocker does not listen to rebuke.

Proverbs 23:24

4. Parents can be exasperating. Children should realize that parents will make mistakes.

Ephesians 6:4 Fathers, do not exasperate your children; instead, bring them up in the training and instruction of the Lord.

Colossians 3:21 Fathers, do not embitter your children, or they will become discouraged.

Colossians 3:13 Bear with each other and forgive whatever grievances you may have against one another. Forgive as the Lord forgave you.

5. You must honor and obey your parents. It is what God commands.

Deuteronomy 5:16 Honor your father and your mother, as the LORD your God has commanded you, so that you may live long and that it may go well with you in the land the LORD your God is giving you.

Ephesians 6:1–2 Children, obey your parents in the Lord, for this is right. "Honor your father and mother"—which is the first commandment with a promise.

6. Disobedience to parents is included in lists of serious sinful behavior.

2 Timothy 3:1–4 But mark this: There will be terrible times in the last days. People will be lovers of themselves, lovers of money, boastful, proud, abusive, disobedient to their parents, ungrateful, unholy, without love, unforgiving, slanderous, without self-control, brutal, not lovers of the good, treacherous, rash, conceited, lovers of pleasure rather than lovers of God.

Romans 1:29–31

7. **The sins of a young person will bring disgrace to parents.**

Proverbs 15:20 A wise son brings joy to his father, but a foolish man despises his mother.

Proverbs 17:25 A foolish son brings grief to his father and bitterness to the one who bore him.

Proverbs 29:3; 30:11

8. **Discipline is difficult but necessary for the youth's proper training.**

Proverbs 3:11–12 My son, do not despise the LORD's discipline and do not resent his rebuke, because the LORD disciplines those he loves, as a father the son he delights in.

Hebrews 12:9–11 Moreover, we have all had human fathers who disciplined us and we respected them for it. How much more should we submit to the Father of our spirits and live! Our fathers disciplined us for a little while as they thought best; but God disciplines us for our good, that we may share in his holiness. No discipline seems pleasant at the time, but painful. Later on, however, it produces a harvest of righteousness and peace for those who have been trained by it.

Proverbs 15:5

9. **Entering into marriage requires that you leave (not forsake or dishonor) your parents. You are to move out and become independent.**

Matthew 19:4–5 "Haven't you read," he replied, "that at the beginning the Creator 'made them male and female,' and said, 'For this reason a man will leave his father and mother and be united to his wife, and the two will become one flesh'?"

10. **When God calls adult children to vocational Christian service, he will sometimes expect them to leave (not forsake or dishonor) their parents for that work. This principle would apply to other careers as well.**

Luke 18:29–30 "I tell you the truth," Jesus said to them, "no one who has left home or wife or brothers or parents or children for the sake of the kingdom of God will fail to receive many times as much in this age and, in the age to come, eternal life."

Mark 1:19–20 When he had gone a little farther, he saw James son of Zebedee and his brother John in a boat, preparing their nets. Without delay he called them, and they left their father Zebedee in the boat with the hired men and followed him.

11. **Children should continue to honor their parents and make sure they are provided for in later years.**

Proverbs 23:22 Listen to your father, who gave you life, and do not despise your mother when she is old.

Leviticus 19:32 Rise in the presence of the aged, show respect for the elderly and revere your God. I am the LORD.

1 Timothy 5:4 But if a widow has children or grandchildren, these should learn first of all to put their religion into practice by caring for their own family and so repaying their parents and grandparents, for this is pleasing to God.

1 Timothy 5:1

Biblical Illustrations—Hophni and Phinehas (1 Samuel 2:22–25); David (1 Samuel 16:11; 17:14–18; 22:3)

Past Memories

See also Bitterness, Guilt, Attitude, Worry

1. **Constantly rehashing past accomplishments, failures, and losses can become a trap. God does not want us trapped by the past.**

   Isaiah 43:18–19 Forget the former things; do not dwell on the past. See, I am doing a new thing! Now it springs up; do you not perceive it? I am making a way in the desert and streams in the wasteland.

   Philippians 3:13–15 Brothers, I do not consider myself yet to have taken hold of it. But one thing I do: Forgetting what is behind and straining toward what is ahead, I press on toward the goal to win the prize for which God has called me heavenward in Christ Jesus. All of us who are mature should take such a view of things. And if on some point you think differently, that too God will make clear to you.

   Luke 9:62

2. **You must focus on God's provision for the past.**

   Psalm 25:6–7 Remember, O LORD, your great mercy and love, for they are from of old. Remember not the sins of my youth and my rebellious ways; according to your love remember me, for you are good, O LORD.

   Psalm 77:11 I will remember the deeds of the LORD; yes, I will remember your miracles of long ago.

   Joshua 21:45; Psalm 68:19; Micah 7:19; Colossians 1:21–23

3. **There is a battle being fought for control of our minds.**

   Psalm 13:2 How long must I wrestle with my thoughts and every day have sorrow in my heart? How long will my enemy triumph over me?

2 Corinthians 10:3–5 For though we live in the world, we do not wage war as the world does. The weapons we fight with are not the weapons of the world. On the contrary, they have divine power to demolish strongholds. We demolish arguments and every pretension that sets itself up against the knowledge of God, and we take captive every thought to make it obedient to Christ.

4. We change our lives by changing how we think.

Psalm 34:4 I sought the LORD, and he answered me; he delivered me from all my fears.

Romans 12:2 Do not conform any longer to the pattern of this world, but be transformed by the renewing of your mind. Then you will be able to test and approve what God's will is—his good, pleasing and perfect will.

Ephesians 4:22–23 You were taught, with regard to your former way of life, to put off your old self, which is being corrupted by its deceitful desires; to be made new in the attitude of your minds.

Philippians 4:6–8

5. Concentrate on what God is doing right now and will do in the future.

Isaiah 42:10 Sing to the LORD a new song, his praise from the ends of the earth, you who go down to the sea, and all that is in it, you islands, and all who live in them.

2 Corinthians 5:17 Therefore, if anyone is in Christ, he is a new creation; the old has gone, the new has come!

Isaiah 26:3

Peer Pressure

See also Choices, Friends, Temptation

1. Doing what is wrong to please others is foolish.

Proverbs 1:10–16 My son, if sinners entice you, do not give in to them. If they say, "Come along with us; let's lie in wait for someone's blood, let's waylay some harmless soul; let's swallow them alive, like the grave, and whole, like those who go down to the pit; we will get all sorts of valuable things and fill our houses with plunder; throw in your lot with us, and we will share a common purse"—my son, do not go along with them, do not set foot on their paths; for their feet rush into sin, they are swift to shed blood.

Proverbs 24:1–2 Do not envy wicked men, do not desire their company; for their hearts plot violence, and their lips talk about making trouble.

2 Peter 2:18–19 For they mouth empty, boastful words and, by appealing to the lustful desires of sinful human nature, they entice people who are just escaping from those who live in error. They promise them freedom, while they themselves are slaves of depravity—for a man is a slave to whatever has mastered him.

2. If peers are influencing you toward what is wrong, stand for what is right.

Ephesians 5:7–11 Therefore do not be partners with them. For you were once darkness, but now you are light in the Lord. Live as children of light (for the fruit of the light consists in all goodness, righteousness and truth) and find out what pleases the Lord. Have nothing to do with the fruitless deeds of darkness, but rather expose them.

1 Corinthians 15:33 Do not be misled: "Bad company corrupts good character."

1 Timothy 4:12 Don't let anyone look down on you because you are young, but set an example for the believers in speech, in life, in love, in faith and in purity.

Ephesians 6:10–11

3. **Moving away from what is wrong is a good start, but we must also move toward what is right.**

2 Timothy 2:22 Flee the evil desires of youth, and pursue righteousness, faith, love and peace, along with those who call on the Lord out of a pure heart.

Biblical Illustration—Herod Antipas (Matthew 14:11–16)

Pornography

See also Thought Life, Lust, Selfishness, Sexual Purity, Temptation

1. **Scripture clearly states that our eyes are to be kept from viewing ungodliness.**

   Psalm 101:3 I will set before my eyes no vile thing. The deeds of faithless men I hate; they will not cling to me.

   Job 31:1 I made a covenant with my eyes not to look lustfully at a girl.

   Isaiah 1:16 Wash and make yourselves clean. Take your evil deeds out of my sight! Stop doing wrong.

   Matthew 5:28 But I tell you that anyone who looks at a woman lustfully has already committed adultery with her in his heart.

2. **Pornography affects one's entire life.**

   Luke 11:34–36 Your eye is the lamp of your body. When your eyes are good, your whole body also is full of light. But when they are bad, your body also is full of darkness. See to it, then, that the light within you is not darkness. Therefore, if your whole body is full of light, and no part of it dark, it will be completely lighted, as when the light of a lamp shines on you.

   James 1:14–15 But each one is tempted when, by his own evil desire, he is dragged away and enticed. Then, after desire has conceived, it gives birth to sin; and sin, when it is full-grown, gives birth to death.

   Proverbs 2:12–15

3. God sees everything; nothing is hidden from him.

Psalm 90:8 You have set our iniquities before you, our secret sins in the light of your presence.

Psalm 139:7–12 Where can I go from your Spirit? Where can I flee from your presence? If I go up to the heavens, you are there; if I make my bed in the depths, you are there. If I rise on the wings of the dawn, if I settle on the far side of the sea, even there your hand will guide me, your right hand will hold me fast. If I say, "Surely the darkness will hide me and the light become night around me," even the darkness will not be dark to you; the night will shine like the day, for darkness is as light to you.

Proverbs 5:21 For a man's ways are in full view of the LORD, and he examines all his paths.

Proverbs 15:3 The eyes of the LORD are everywhere, keeping watch on the wicked and the good.

Proverbs 15:11

4. It is vital to turn from this sin and remove pornography entirely from one's life.

Psalm 32:3–5 When I kept silent, my bones wasted away through my groaning all day long. For day and night your hand was heavy upon me; my strength was sapped as in the heat of summer. Then I acknowledged my sin to you and did not cover up my iniquity. I said, "I will confess my transgressions to the LORD"—and you forgave the guilt of my sin.

Psalm 119:37 Turn my eyes away from worthless things; preserve my life according to your word.

Romans 13:14 Rather, clothe yourselves with the Lord Jesus Christ, and do not think about how to gratify the desires of the sinful nature.

Galatians 5:16 So I say, live by the Spirit, and you will not gratify the desires of the sinful nature.

Psalm 139:23–24; Romans 6:1–13; 1 Peter 2:24

5. Seek accountability with those who have maturity in this area.

2 Timothy 2:21–22 If a man cleanses himself from the latter, he will be an instrument for noble purposes, made holy, useful to the Master and prepared to do any good work. Flee the evil desires of youth, and pursue righteousness, faith, love and peace, along with those who call on the Lord out of a pure heart.

Galatians 6:1–2 Brothers, if someone is caught in a sin, you who are spiritual should restore him gently. But watch yourself, or you also may be tempted. Carry each other's burdens, and in this way you will fulfill the law of Christ.

2 Chronicles 16:9 For the eyes of the LORD range throughout the earth to strengthen those whose hearts are fully committed to him.

Prayer

1. **Prayer is the Christian's lifeline. We must pray—consistently and constantly!**

   Psalm 55:17 Evening, morning and noon I cry out in distress, and he hears my voice.

   Psalm 86:3, 7 Have mercy on me, O Lord, for I call to you all day long. . . . In the day of my trouble I will call to you, for you will answer me.

   Luke 18:1 Then Jesus told his disciples a parable to show them that they should always pray and not give up.

   1 Thessalonians 5:17 Pray continually.

   Matthew 7:7; Ephesians 6:18

2. **We must pray in Jesus's name, that is, according to his holiness and character.**

   John 14:13 And I will do whatever you ask in my name, so that the Son may bring glory to the Father.

   John 15:16 You did not choose me, but I chose you and appointed you to go and bear fruit—fruit that will last. Then the Father will give you whatever you ask in my name.

3. **Sin can hinder our prayers.**

   Psalm 66:18 If I had cherished sin in my heart, the Lord would not have listened.

   Isaiah 59:1–2 Surely the arm of the Lord is not too short to save, nor his ear too dull to hear. But your iniquities have separated you from your God; your sins have hidden his face from you, so that he will not hear.

4. As Jesus's disciples did, we should ask that he teach us how to pray.

Luke 11:1 One day Jesus was praying in a certain place. When he finished, one of his disciples said to him, "Lord, teach us to pray, just as John taught his disciples."

5. Our motivation must be to advance God's kingdom and his glory, not our selfish desires.

Luke 11:2 He said to them, "When you pray, say: 'Father, hallowed be your name, your kingdom come.'"

1 John 5:14–15 This is the confidence we have in approaching God: that if we ask anything according to his will, he hears us. And if we know that he hears us—whatever we ask—we know that we have what we asked of him.

6. We can pray about anything that concerns us.

Philippians 4:6–7 Do not be anxious about anything, but in everything, by prayer and petition, with thanksgiving, present your requests to God. And the peace of God, which transcends all understanding, will guard your hearts and your minds in Christ Jesus.

7. Our Father in heaven desires to give us what is good.

Matthew 7:7–11 Ask and it will be given to you; seek and you will find; knock and the door will be opened to you. For everyone who asks receives; he who seeks finds; and to him who knocks, the door will be opened. Which of you, if his son asks for bread, will give him a stone? Or if he asks for a fish, will give him a snake? If you, then, though you are evil, know how to give good gifts to your children, how much more will your Father in heaven give good gifts to those who ask him!

Biblical Illustrations—Abraham's servant (Genesis 24); Nehemiah (Nehemiah 1); Daniel (Daniel 6); Jesus (Matthew 6:9–13; 14:23; Mark 1:35; Luke 5:16; John 17)

Pride/Humility

See also Complaining

1. Humility is pleasing to God; he hates sinful pride.

Proverbs 8:13 To fear the LORD is to hate evil; I hate pride and arrogance, evil behavior and perverse speech.

James 4:6 But he gives us more grace. That is why Scripture says: "God opposes the proud but gives grace to the humble."

Psalm 138:6; Proverbs 3:34

2. Sinful pride brings only negative results.

Proverbs 13:10 Pride only breeds quarrels, but wisdom is found in those who take advice.

Proverbs 16:18 Pride goes before destruction, a haughty spirit before a fall.

Isaiah 2:11 The eyes of the arrogant man will be humbled and the pride of men brought low; the LORD alone will be exalted in that day.

Psalm 18:27; Mark 7:20–23

3. There is a type of boasting that pleases God.

Jeremiah 9:23–24 This is what the LORD says: "Let not the wise man boast of his wisdom or the strong man boast of his strength or the rich man boast of his riches, but let him who boasts boast about this: that he understands and knows me, that I am the LORD, who exercises kindness, justice and righteousness on earth, for in these I delight," declares the LORD.

Psalm 44:8 In God we make our boast all day long, and we will praise your name forever.

Galatians 6:14 May I never boast except in the cross of our Lord Jesus Christ, through which the world has been crucified to me, and I to the world.

4. **We must recognize that God is the source of all we have and can do.**

John 15:5 I am the vine; you are the branches. If a man remains in me and I in him, he will bear much fruit; apart from me you can do nothing.

1 Timothy 6:17 Command those who are rich in this present world not to be arrogant nor to put their hope in wealth, which is so uncertain, but to put their hope in God, who richly provides us with everything for our enjoyment.

5. **Pride must be replaced by humility.**

Philippians 2:3 Do nothing out of selfish ambition or vain conceit, but in humility consider others better than yourselves.

Romans 12:3 For by the grace given me I say to every one of you: Do not think of yourself more highly than you ought, but rather think of yourself with sober judgment, in accordance with the measure of faith God has given you.

1 Peter 5:5 Young men, in the same way be submissive to those who are older. All of you, clothe yourselves with humility toward one another, because, "God opposes the proud but gives grace to the humble."

Matthew 20:26–28; 1 John 2:15–17

Biblical Illustrations—Joseph (Genesis 37:5–8); Nebuchadnezzar (Daniel 4:28–37); Jesus (John 13; Philippians 2:5–8); Paul (2 Corinthians 12:1–10; Philippians 3:4–8)

Profanity

See also Speech

1. **Since the name of God represents who he is in his holy character and perfection, we must be careful not to speak that name in a profane (i.e., common) manner. We must not cheapen his holy name.**

   Exodus 20:7 You shall not misuse the name of the LORD your God, for the LORD will not hold anyone guiltless who misuses his name.

   Psalm 74:18 Remember how the enemy has mocked you, O LORD, how foolish people have reviled your name.

   Psalm 8:1 O LORD, our Lord, how majestic is your name in all the earth! You have set your glory above the heavens.

   Leviticus 19:12

2. **Proper respect is due the name of God, never the flippant "Oh my God" or "By God."**

   Luke 11:2 He said to them, "When you pray, say: 'Father, hallowed be your name, your kingdom come.'"

   Jeremiah 10:6–7 No one is like you, O LORD; you are great, and your name is mighty in power. Who should not revere you, O King of the nations? This is your due. Among all the wise men of the nations and in all their kingdoms, there is no one like you.

   Psalm 138:2

3. **God is not pleased with coarse and perverted speech.**

   Proverbs 12:13–14 An evil man is trapped by his sinful talk, but a righteous man escapes trouble. From the fruit of his lips a man is filled with good things as surely as the work of his hands rewards him.

Ephesians 4:29–30 Do not let any unwholesome talk come out of your mouths, but only what is helpful for building others up according to their needs, that it may benefit those who listen. And do not grieve the Holy Spirit of God, with whom you were sealed for the day of redemption.

Proverbs 8:13; Matthew 15:18–19

4. Christians should be separated from speech that is foul and perverted.

Psalm 1:1 Blessed is the man who does not walk in the counsel of the wicked or stand in the way of sinners or sit in the seat of mockers.

Psalm 39:1 I said, "I will watch my ways and keep my tongue from sin; I will put a muzzle on my mouth as long as the wicked are in my presence."

Psalm 17:3 Though you probe my heart and examine me at night, though you test me, you will find nothing; I have resolved that my mouth will not sin.

Proverbs 10:31–32; James 3:8–11

Prostitution

See also Lust, Confession, Sexual Purity

1. **Being involved in or soliciting prostitution is immoral and a desecration of the body.**

    1 Corinthians 6:15–20 Do you not know that your bodies are members of Christ himself? Shall I then take the members of Christ and unite them with a prostitute? Never! Do you not know that he who unites himself with a prostitute is one with her in body? For it is said, "The two will become one flesh." But he who unites himself with the Lord is one with him in spirit. Flee from sexual immorality. All other sins a man commits are outside his body, but he who sins sexually sins against his own body. Do you not know that your body is a temple of the Holy Spirit, who is in you, whom you have received from God? You are not your own; you were bought at a price. Therefore honor God with your body.

2. **Prostitution is never an option.**

    Proverbs 6:24–25 Keeping you from the immoral woman, from the smooth tongue of the wayward wife. Do not lust in your heart after her beauty or let her captivate you with her eyes, for the prostitute reduces you to a loaf of bread, and the adulteress preys upon your very life.

    Proverbs 2:16–19

3. **God is ready to forgive any sin, including prostitution.**

    1 John 1:9 If we confess our sins, he is faithful and just and will forgive us our sins and purify us from all unrighteousness.

1 Corinthians 6:9–11 Do you not know that the wicked will not inherit the kingdom of God? Do not be deceived: Neither the sexually immoral nor idolaters nor adulterers nor male prostitutes nor homosexual offenders nor thieves nor the greedy nor drunkards nor slanderers nor swindlers will inherit the kingdom of God. And that is what some of you were. But you were washed, you were sanctified, you were justified in the name of the Lord Jesus Christ and by the Spirit of our God.

Micah 7:18–19 Who is a God like you, who pardons sin and forgives the transgression of the remnant of his inheritance? You do not stay angry forever but delight to show mercy. You will again have compassion on us; you will tread our sins underfoot and hurl all our iniquities into the depths of the sea.

Biblical Illustrations—Rahab (Joshua 2); parable of two sisters (Ezekiel 23); prodigal son (Luke 15)

Puberty

See also Self-Worth, Self-Control

1. **God made us as we are—male and female. Differences in the sexes were his idea. The changes that come are good, according to his design.**

   Genesis 1:27 So God created man in his own image, in the image of God he created him; male and female he created them.

   Genesis 2:21–23 So the LORD God caused the man to fall into a deep sleep; and while he was sleeping, he took one of the man's ribs and closed up the place with flesh. Then the LORD God made a woman from the rib he had taken out of the man, and he brought her to the man. The man said, "This is now bone of my bones and flesh of my flesh; she shall be called 'woman,' for she was taken out of man."

2. **Jesus developed from a youth to an adult.**

   Luke 2:52 And Jesus grew in wisdom and stature, and in favor with God and men.

3. **With maturity comes new responsibility.**

   1 Corinthians 13:11 When I was a child, I talked like a child, I thought like a child, I reasoned like a child. When I became a man, I put childish ways behind me.

   1 Timothy 4:12 Don't let anyone look down on you because you are young, but set an example for the believers in speech, in life, in love, in faith and in purity.

   Psalm 71:5 For you have been my hope, O Sovereign LORD, my confidence since my youth.

Jeremiah 1:7 But the LORD said to me, "Do not say, 'I am only a child.' You must go to everyone I send you to and say whatever I command you."

Biblical Illustrations—Rebekah (Genesis 24); David (1 Samuel 17); Daniel (Daniel 1); Jeremiah (Jeremiah 1)

Quiet Time

1. Meeting with God alone each day is essential.

Ecclesiastes 12:1 Remember your Creator in the days of your youth, before the days of trouble come and the years approach when you will say, "I find no pleasure in them."

Deuteronomy 32:47 They are not just idle words for you—they are your life.

Psalm 42:1–2 As the deer pants for streams of water, so my soul pants for you, O God. My soul thirsts for God, for the living God. When can I go and meet with God?

Psalm 63:1

2. Time in God's Word—reading, studying, and memorizing it—gives guidance for the issues of life.

Joshua 1:8 Do not let this Book of the Law depart from your mouth; meditate on it day and night, so that you may be careful to do everything written in it. Then you will be prosperous and successful.

Psalm 119:9–11 How can a young man keep his way pure? By living according to your word. I seek you with all my heart; do not let me stray from your commands. I have hidden your word in my heart that I might not sin against you.

Psalm 19:9–11 The fear of the LORD is pure, enduring forever. The ordinances of the LORD are sure and altogether righteous. They are more precious than gold, than much pure gold; they are sweeter than honey, than honey from the comb. By them is your servant warned; in keeping them there is great reward.

Hebrews 4:12 For the word of God is living and active. Sharper than any double-edged sword, it penetrates even to dividing soul and spirit, joints and marrow; it judges the thoughts and attitudes of the heart.

Psalm 1:2–3; 119:105, 129–30; Isaiah 55:11; 2 Timothy 3:16–17

3. Spending time daily in prayer is essential.

Psalm 88:13 But I cry to you for help, O Lord; in the morning my prayer comes before you.

Psalm 119:147–48 I rise before dawn and cry for help; I have put my hope in your word. My eyes stay open through the watches of the night, that I may meditate on your promises.

Ephesians 6:18 And pray in the Spirit on all occasions with all kinds of prayers and requests. With this in mind, be alert and always keep on praying for all the saints.

Psalm 5:2–3; Jeremiah 33:3; Hebrews 4:16

4. Examples in Scripture.

Ezra 7:10 For Ezra had devoted himself to the study and observance of the Law of the Lord, and to teaching its decrees and laws in Israel.

Daniel 6:10 Three times a day he got down on his knees and prayed, giving thanks to his God, just as he had done before.

Habakkuk 2:1 I will stand at my watch and station myself on the ramparts; I will look to see what he will say to me, and what answer I am to give to this complaint.

Matthew 14:23 After he had dismissed them, he went up on a mountainside by himself to pray. When evening came, he was there alone.

Mark 1:35 Very early in the morning, while it was still dark, Jesus got up, left the house and went off to a solitary place, where he prayed.

Luke 5:16 But Jesus often withdrew to lonely places and prayed.

Rape

See also Bitterness, Fear, Forgiving Others, Past Memories

1. **When rape happens, God does not place blame on the person raped.**

   Deuteronomy 22:26 Do nothing to the girl; she has committed no sin deserving death.

2. **God hates the violent actions of wicked people.**

   Proverbs 6:16–18 There are six things the Lord hates, seven that are detestable to him: haughty eyes, a lying tongue, hands that shed innocent blood, a heart that devises wicked schemes, feet that are quick to rush into evil.

3. **When such evil happens, courts and laws may not always be able to provide justice, but God ultimately will.**

   Deuteronomy 32:35 It is mine to avenge; I will repay. In due time their foot will slip; their day of disaster is near and their doom rushes upon them.

   Luke 18:6–8

4. **Seek God's justice, not revenge.**

   Romans 12:19 Do not take revenge, my friends, but leave room for God's wrath, for it is written: "It is mine to avenge; I will repay," says the Lord.

   Romans 13:3–4 For rulers hold no terror for those who do right, but for those who do wrong. Do you want to be free from fear of the one in authority? Then do what is right and he will commend you. For he is God's servant to do you good. But if you do wrong, be afraid, for he does not bear the sword for nothing. He is God's servant, an agent of wrath to bring punishment on the wrongdoer.

5. Cling to your heavenly Father for relief.

Psalm 10:17–18 You hear, O Lord, the desire of the afflicted; you encourage them, and you listen to their cry, defending the fatherless and the oppressed, in order that man, who is of the earth, may terrify no more.

Isaiah 25:4 You have been a refuge for the poor, a refuge for the needy in his distress, a shelter from the storm and a shade from the heat. For the breath of the ruthless is like a storm driving against a wall.

Isaiah 43:1–2 Fear not, for I have redeemed you; I have summoned you by name; you are mine. When you pass through the waters, I will be with you; and when you pass through the rivers, they will not sweep over you.

Deuteronomy 31:6; Psalm 34:18–19; Isaiah 41:9–10

Note: It would be beneficial to have the counselee see a physician, pastor, or trained biblical counselor. Counselors must report rape as required by law.

Runaways

See also Authority, Bitterness, Abuse, Depression, Loneliness

1. **If tempted to run away, go to your parents or to Christian leaders for help. If parents themselves are the source of the problem, Christian leaders can assist in improving your relationship with them.**

   Deuteronomy 5:16 Honor your father and your mother, as the LORD your God has commanded you, so that you may live long and that it may go well with you in the land the LORD your God is giving you.

   Proverbs 1:8–9 Listen, my son, to your father's instruction and do not forsake your mother's teaching. They will be a garland to grace your head and a chain to adorn your neck.

   Proverbs 15:22 Plans fail for lack of counsel, but with many advisers they succeed.

   Hebrews 13:7 Remember your leaders, who spoke the word of God to you. Consider the outcome of their way of life and imitate their faith.

2. **God can handle any problem that comes your way. He is always with you.**

   Psalm 61:1–4 Hear my cry, O God; listen to my prayer. From the ends of the earth I call to you, I call as my heart grows faint; lead me to the rock that is higher than I. For you have been my refuge, a strong tower against the foe. I long to dwell in your tent forever and take refuge in the shelter of your wings.

   Proverbs 2:6 For the LORD gives wisdom, and from his mouth come knowledge and understanding.

   Isaiah 43:1–2

3. God's love is never ending.

Lamentations 3:21–23 Yet this I call to mind and therefore I have hope: Because of the LORD's great love we are not consumed, for his compassions never fail. They are new every morning; great is your faithfulness.

Romans 8:38–39 I am convinced that neither death nor life, neither angels nor demons, neither the present nor the future, nor any powers, neither height nor depth, nor anything else in all creation, will be able to separate us from the love of God that is in Christ Jesus our Lord.

Romans 5:8; Ephesians 2:4–5

4. No matter what sins you have committed, God is gracious to forgive. You can come back to God and home.

Isaiah 1:18 "Come now, let us reason together," says the LORD. "Though your sins are like scarlet, they shall be as white as snow; though they are red as crimson, they shall be like wool."

Psalm 103:12 As far as the east is from the west, so far has he removed our transgressions from us.

Micah 7:18–19 Who is a God like you, who pardons sin and forgives the transgression of the remnant of his inheritance? You do not stay angry forever but delight to show mercy. You will again have compassion on us; you will tread our sins underfoot and hurl all our iniquities into the depths of the sea.

5. Most parents will gladly welcome their child back home.

Luke 15:20, 32 So he got up and went to his father. But while he was still a long way off, his father saw him and was filled with compassion for him; he ran to his son, threw his arms around him and kissed him. . . . "But we had to celebrate and be glad, because this brother of yours was dead and is alive again; he was lost and is found."

Luke 15:4–6 Suppose one of you has a hundred sheep and loses one of them. Does he not leave the ninety-nine in the open country and go after the lost sheep until he finds it? And when he finds it, he joyfully puts it on his shoulders and goes home. Then he calls his friends and neighbors together and says, "Rejoice with me; I have found my lost sheep."

Self-Control

1. Lack of self-control leads to attacks from Satan and to broken lives.

1 Peter 5:8 Be self-controlled and alert. Your enemy the devil prowls around like a roaring lion looking for someone to devour.

Proverbs 25:28 Like a city whose walls are broken down is a man who lacks self-control.

2. Lack of self-control is included in lists of sins to avoid.

2 Timothy 3:1–5 But mark this: There will be terrible times in the last days. People will be lovers of themselves, lovers of money, boastful, proud, abusive, disobedient to their parents, ungrateful, unholy, without love, unforgiving, slanderous, without self-control, brutal, not lovers of the good, treacherous, rash, conceited, lovers of pleasure rather than lovers of God—having a form of godliness but denying its power. Have nothing to do with them.

Galatians 5:19–21 The acts of the sinful nature are obvious: sexual immorality, impurity and debauchery; idolatry and witchcraft; hatred, discord, jealousy, fits of rage, selfish ambition, dissensions, factions and envy; drunkenness, orgies, and the like. I warn you, as I did before, that those who live like this will not inherit the kingdom of God.

3. Possessing self-control is included in lists of positive Christian qualities.

Galatians 5:22–23 But the fruit of the Spirit is love, joy, peace, patience, kindness, goodness, faithfulness, gentleness and self-control. Against such things there is no law.

2 Peter 1:5–6 For this very reason, make every effort to add to your faith goodness; and to goodness, knowledge; and to knowledge, self-control; and to self-control, perseverance; and to perseverance, godliness.

4. The lifestyle of mature Christians includes self-control.

1 Thessalonians 5:5–8 You are all sons of the light and sons of the day. We do not belong to the night or to the darkness. So then, let us not be like others, who are asleep, but let us be alert and self-controlled. For those who sleep, sleep at night, and those who get drunk, get drunk at night. But since we belong to the day, let us be self-controlled, putting on faith and love as a breastplate, and the hope of salvation as a helmet.

1 Peter 1:13–16 Therefore, prepare your minds for action; be self-controlled; set your hope fully on the grace to be given you when Jesus Christ is revealed. As obedient children, do not conform to the evil desires you had when you lived in ignorance. But just as he who called you is holy, so be holy in all you do; for it is written: "Be holy, because I am holy."

Self-Injury/Cutting

See also Self-Worth, Suicide, Temptation

1. **When life seems out of control, going to God is the answer, not doing something that gives a temporary feeling of control followed by guilt.**

   Deuteronomy 13:4 It is the LORD your God you must follow, and him you must revere. Keep his commands and obey him; serve him and hold fast to him.

   Titus 2:11–12 For the grace of God that brings salvation has appeared to all men. It teaches us to say "No" to ungodliness and worldly passions, and to live self-controlled, upright and godly lives in this present age.

   Colossians 3:2–3 Set your minds on things above, not on earthly things. For you died, and your life is now hidden with Christ in God.

   Philippians 3:8

2. **God does not want us to hurt or damage our bodies, his temple.**

   Leviticus 19:28 Do not cut your bodies for the dead or put tattoo marks on yourselves. I am the LORD.

   Leviticus 20:23 You must not live according to the customs of the nations I am going to drive out before you. Because they did all these things, I abhorred them.

   1 Corinthians 6:19–20 Do you not know that your body is a temple of the Holy Spirit, who is in you, whom you have received from God?

You are not your own; you were bought at a price. Therefore honor God with your body.

Ephesians 4:17–20

3. Self-injury is a trap Satan uses to cause us to lose confidence in God and give up his blessing.

2 Corinthians 11:3 But I am afraid that just as Eve was deceived by the serpent's cunning, your minds may somehow be led astray from your sincere and pure devotion to Christ.

Ephesians 6:11–13

4. The false peace that comes from self-injury is fleeting—true peace is lasting and genuine.

John 14:27 Peace I leave with you; my peace I give you. I do not give to you as the world gives. Do not let your hearts be troubled and do not be afraid.

Colossians 3:15–17 Let the peace of Christ rule in your hearts, since as members of one body you were called to peace. And be thankful. Let the word of Christ dwell in you richly as you teach and admonish one another with all wisdom, and as you sing psalms, hymns and spiritual songs with gratitude in your hearts to God. And whatever you do, whether in word or deed, do it all in the name of the Lord Jesus, giving thanks to God the Father through him.

Psalm 34:18; Romans 5:1

5. Change happens when we choose to think as God thinks about self-injury.

Galatians 5:24 Those who belong to Christ Jesus have crucified the sinful nature with its passions and desires.

Romans 12:2 Do not conform any longer to the pattern of this world, but be transformed by the renewing of your mind. Then you will be able to test and approve what God's will is—his good, pleasing and perfect will.

Colossians 3:5 Put to death, therefore, whatever belongs to your earthly nature: sexual immorality, impurity, lust, evil desires and greed, which is idolatry.

6. Submission to God and what he requires is crucial.

Ecclesiastes 12:1 Remember your Creator in the days of your youth, before the days of trouble come and the years approach when you will say, "I find no pleasure in them."

Ecclesiastes 12:14 For God will bring every deed into judgment, including every hidden thing, whether it is good or evil.

James 4:7 Submit yourselves, then, to God. Resist the devil, and he will flee from you.

Ephesians 4:30

7. God is greater than the temptation.

1 Corinthians 10:13 No temptation has seized you except what is common to man. And God is faithful; he will not let you be tempted beyond what you can bear. But when you are tempted, he will also provide a way out so that you can stand up under it.

Philippians 1:6 Being confident of this, that he who began a good work in you will carry it on to completion until the day of Christ Jesus.

1 John 4:4 You, dear children, are from God and have overcome them, because the one who is in you is greater than the one who is in the world.

Biblical Illustration—Elijah and the prophets of Baal (1 Kings 18)

Note: It would be beneficial to have the counselee see a physician, pastor, or trained biblical counselor.

Selfishness/Others First

See also Compassion, Pride

1. Selfishness is a sin and beneficial to no one.

James 3:14–16 But if you harbor bitter envy and selfish ambition in your hearts, do not boast about it or deny the truth. Such "wisdom" does not come down from heaven but is earthly, unspiritual, of the devil. For where you have envy and selfish ambition, there you find disorder and every evil practice.

Romans 2:8 But for those who are self-seeking and who reject the truth and follow evil, there will be wrath and anger.

2. God expects us to place him first.

Matthew 22:37–38 Jesus replied: "Love the Lord your God with all your heart and with all your soul and with all your mind. This is the first and greatest commandment."

Luke 9:23–24 Then he said to them all: "If anyone would come after me, he must deny himself and take up his cross daily and follow me. For whoever wants to save his life will lose it, but whoever loses his life for me will save it."

Matthew 6:33

3. God expects us to place others ahead of ourselves.

Philippians 2:3–4 Do nothing out of selfish ambition or vain conceit, but in humility consider others better than yourselves. Each of you should look not only to your own interests, but also to the interests of others.

1 Corinthians 10:24 Nobody should seek his own good, but the good of others.

1 Corinthians 13:4–5 Love is patient, love is kind. It does not envy, it does not boast, it is not proud. It is not rude, it is not self-seeking, it is not easily angered, it keeps no record of wrongs.

Romans 15:1–3 We who are strong ought to bear with the failings of the weak and not to please ourselves. Each of us should please his neighbor for his good, to build him up. For even Christ did not please himself but, as it is written: "The insults of those who insult you have fallen on me."

Romans 12:10; Ephesians 5:21

Biblical Illustrations—Negative: Lot (Genesis 13); Jacob (Genesis 27); shepherds of Israel (Ezekiel 34); James and John (Mark 10:35–45). Positive: Jonathan (1 Samuel 19–20); Paul (Romans 9:1–3); Jesus (Philippians 2:5–8)

Self-Worth

1. **Every human being is made in the image of God, according to his design.**

   Genesis 1:27 So God created man in his own image, in the image of God he created him; male and female he created them.

   Genesis 2:21–22 So the LORD God caused the man to fall into a deep sleep; and while he was sleeping, he took one of the man's ribs and closed up the place with flesh. Then the LORD God made a woman from the rib he had taken out of the man, and he brought her to the man.

   Luke 12:7 Indeed, the very hairs of your head are all numbered. Don't be afraid; you are worth more than many sparrows.

   Genesis 2:7; Psalm 139:13–16

2. **God sending his Son to die for us shows his view of our self-worth.**

   John 3:16 For God so loved the world that he gave his one and only Son, that whoever believes in him shall not perish but have eternal life.

   Romans 5:8 But God demonstrates his own love for us in this: While we were still sinners, Christ died for us.

   1 Peter 2:9

3. **Christians must find significance in their relationship to God, not in themselves or in others.**

   John 15:15 I no longer call you servants, because a servant does not know his master's business. Instead, I have called you friends, for everything that I learned from my Father I have made known to you.

Ephesians 1:18–19 I pray also that the eyes of your heart may be enlightened in order that you may know the hope to which he has called you, the riches of his glorious inheritance in the saints, and his incomparably great power for us who believe. That power is like the working of his mighty strength.

Ephesians 2:6–7 And God raised us up with Christ and seated us with him in the heavenly realms in Christ Jesus, in order that in the coming ages he might show the incomparable riches of his grace, expressed in his kindness to us in Christ Jesus.

Isaiah 41:9; Jeremiah 31:3; Micah 6:8

4. Knowing God is what makes life meaningful.

Jeremiah 9:23–24 This is what the LORD says: "Let not the wise man boast of his wisdom or the strong man boast of his strength or the rich man boast of his riches, but let him who boasts boast about this: that he understands and knows me, that I am the LORD, who exercises kindness, justice and righteousness on earth, for in these I delight," declares the LORD.

Ephesians 3:14–20; Philippians 3:8–10

5. Relying on self can be a dangerous trap.

Romans 12:3 For by the grace given me I say to every one of you: Do not think of yourself more highly than you ought, but rather think of yourself with sober judgment, in accordance with the measure of faith God has given you.

2 Corinthians 1:8–9 We do not want you to be uninformed, brothers, about the hardships we suffered in the province of Asia. We were under great pressure, far beyond our ability to endure, so that we despaired even of life. Indeed, in our hearts we felt the sentence of death. But this happened that we might not rely on ourselves but on God, who raises the dead.

Biblical Illustrations—Elijah (1 Kings 19:4, 10); Job (Job 3:11; 9:21); David (Psalm 22:6; 31:11)

Sexual Purity

See also Confession, Entertainment, Temptation, Lust, Thought Life

1. Our bodies belong to God; he requires purity.

1 Corinthians 6:18–20 Flee from sexual immorality. All other sins a man commits are outside his body, but he who sins sexually sins against his own body. Do you not know that your body is a temple of the Holy Spirit, who is in you, whom you have received from God? You are not your own; you were bought at a price. Therefore honor God with your body.

Romans 6:13 Do not offer the parts of your body to sin, as instruments of wickedness, but rather offer yourselves to God, as those who have been brought from death to life; and offer the parts of your body to him as instruments of righteousness.

1 Peter 1:16 For it is written: "Be holy, because I am holy."

Matthew 5:8

2. Guard purity of the mind as well as the body.

Matthew 5:28 But I tell you that anyone who looks at a woman lustfully has already committed adultery with her in his heart.

Job 31:1 I made a covenant with my eyes not to look lustfully at a girl.

Psalm 101:3 I will set before my eyes no vile thing. The deeds of faithless men I hate; they will not cling to me.

Philippians 4:8

3. Each person must make good choices to stay pure.

1 Peter 2:11 Dear friends, I urge you, as aliens and strangers in the world, to abstain from sinful desires, which war against your soul.

James 1:14 But each one is tempted when, by his own evil desire, he is dragged away and enticed.

4. Treat others with respect and purity. They will likely be someone's husband or someone's wife one day.

1 Timothy 5:1–2 Do not rebuke an older man harshly, but exhort him as if he were your father. Treat younger men as brothers, older women as mothers, and younger women as sisters, with absolute purity.

5. Be determined and committed, with God's help, to stand strong.

Isaiah 50:7 Because the Sovereign LORD helps me, I will not be disgraced. Therefore have I set my face like flint, and I know I will not be put to shame.

6. Protecting purity in marriage begins long before the wedding.

Hebrews 13:4 Marriage should be honored by all, and the marriage bed kept pure, for God will judge the adulterer and all the sexually immoral.

7. Sexual immorality is wrong and needs to be avoided. It is sinful, period.

Galatians 5:19–20 The acts of the sinful nature are obvious: sexual immorality, impurity and debauchery; idolatry and witchcraft; hatred, discord, jealousy, fits of rage, selfish ambition, dissensions, factions.

1 Thessalonians 4:3–4 It is God's will that you should be sanctified: that you should avoid sexual immorality; that each of you should learn to control his own body in a way that is holy and honorable.

Romans 13:13–14 Let us behave decently, as in the daytime, not in orgies and drunkenness, not in sexual immorality and debauchery, not in dissension and jealousy. Rather, clothe yourselves with the

Lord Jesus Christ, and do not think about how to gratify the desires of the sinful nature.

8. Do not even get close to sexual impurity.

Ephesians 5:3 But among you there must not be even a hint of sexual immorality, or of any kind of impurity, or of greed, because these are improper for God's holy people.

Proverbs 6:27 Can a man scoop fire into his lap without his clothes being burned?

9. Do not submit to pressure sexually or in any other area.

Isaiah 51:7 Hear me, you who know what is right, you people who have my law in your hearts: Do not fear the reproach of men or be terrified by their insults.

1 Corinthians 10:13 No temptation has seized you except what is common to man. And God is faithful; he will not let you be tempted beyond what you can bear. But when you are tempted, he will also provide a way out so that you can stand up under it.

10. Avoid immorality by pursuing what is pure.

2 Timothy 2:22 Flee the evil desires of youth, and pursue righteousness, faith, love and peace, along with those who call on the Lord out of a pure heart.

Proverbs 4; 5; 7; 9; Romans 8:5–6

11. There is no sin that God will not forgive completely.

Psalm 86:5 You are forgiving and good, O Lord, abounding in love to all who call to you.

Romans 8:1–2 Therefore, there is now no condemnation for those who are in Christ Jesus, because through Christ Jesus the law of the Spirit of life set me free from the law of sin and death.

Isaiah 38:17 Surely it was for my benefit that I suffered such anguish. In your love you kept me from the pit of destruction; you have put all my sins behind your back.

Isaiah 43:25 I, even I, am he who blots out your transgressions, for my own sake, and remembers your sins no more.

Psalm 130:3–4; Isaiah 44:22; Lamentations 3:22; Micah 7:18–19; Colossians 1:14

Biblical Illustration—Joseph (Genesis 39:1–23)

Sibling Rivalry

See also Anger, Forgiving Others, Selfishness

1. **The model of love in the body of Christ should be the pattern for families.**

   Romans 12:10 Be devoted to one another in brotherly love. Honor one another above yourselves.

   1 Peter 1:22 Now that you have purified yourselves by obeying the truth so that you have sincere love for your brothers, love one another deeply, from the heart.

   2 Peter 1:5–7 For this very reason, make every effort to add to your faith goodness; and to goodness, knowledge; and to knowledge, self-control; and to self-control, perseverance; and to perseverance, godliness; and to godliness, brotherly kindness; and to brotherly kindness, love.

   Hebrews 13:1; 1 John 4:19–21

2. **Family life should reflect Christian life.**

   Proverbs 19:11 A man's wisdom gives him patience; it is to his glory to overlook an offense.

   Matthew 7:3–5 Why do you look at the speck of sawdust in your brother's eye and pay no attention to the plank in your own eye? How can you say to your brother, "Let me take the speck out of your eye," when all the time there is a plank in your own eye? You hypocrite, first take the plank out of your own eye, and then you will see clearly to remove the speck from your brother's eye.

   1 Thessalonians 5:15 Make sure that nobody pays back wrong for wrong, but always try to be kind to each other and to everyone else.

193

1 Peter 3:8–9 Finally, all of you, live in harmony with one another; be sympathetic, love as brothers, be compassionate and humble. Do not repay evil with evil or insult with insult, but with blessing, because to this you were called so that you may inherit a blessing.

Romans 12:21

3. "Others first" is a rule of life, especially in the family.

Philippians 2:3–4 Do nothing out of selfish ambition or vain conceit, but in humility consider others better than yourselves. Each of you should look not only to your own interests, but also to the interests of others.

Luke 6:31 Do to others as you would have them do to you.

Matthew 5:38–42; Ephesians 5:21

4. Peacemaking should always be a priority.

Matthew 5:9 Blessed are the peacemakers, for they will be called sons of God.

Romans 14:19 Let us therefore make every effort to do what leads to peace and to mutual edification.

Romans 12:18

5. Wise use of our speech helps keep peace with brothers and sisters.

Proverbs 15:1 A gentle answer turns away wrath, but a harsh word stirs up anger.

Proverbs 15:4 The tongue that brings healing is a tree of life, but a deceitful tongue crushes the spirit.

James 5:9 Don't grumble against each other, brothers, or you will be judged. The Judge is standing at the door!

Proverbs 6:16–19; James 4:11

Biblical Illustration—Joseph (Genesis 50)

Singleness

See also Friends, Loneliness, Sexual Purity, Dating

1. Paul presents the single life as a viable option.

1 Corinthians 7:1, 8–9 Now for the matters you wrote about: It is good for a man not to marry. . . . Now to the unmarried and the widows I say: "It is good for them to stay unmarried, as I am. But if they cannot control themselves, they should marry, for it is better to marry than to burn with passion."

2. Singleness is the gift of living undivided for the Lord.

Matthew 19:11–12 Jesus replied, "Not everyone can accept this word, but only those to whom it has been given. For some are eunuchs because they were born that way; others were made that way by men; and others have renounced marriage because of the kingdom of heaven. The one who can accept this should accept it."

1 Corinthians 7:25–28, 32–35 Now about virgins: I have no command from the Lord, but I give a judgment as one who by the Lord's mercy is trustworthy. Because of the present crisis, I think that it is good for you to remain as you are. Are you married? Do not seek a divorce. Are you unmarried? Do not look for a wife. But if you do marry, you have not sinned; and if a virgin marries, she has not sinned. But those who marry will face many troubles in this life, and I want to spare you this. . . . I would like you to be free from concern. An unmarried man is concerned about the Lord's affairs—how he can please the Lord. But a married man is concerned about the affairs of this world—how he can please his wife—and his interests are divided. An unmarried woman or virgin is concerned about the Lord's affairs: Her aim is to be devoted to the Lord in both body and spirit. But a married woman is concerned about the affairs of this world—how she can please her husband. I am saying this for your own good, not to restrict you, but that you may live in a right way in undivided devotion to the Lord.

Being Content with the Single Life

1. God always has our best interests at heart.

Jeremiah 29:11 "For I know the plans I have for you," declares the Lord, "plans to prosper you and not to harm you, plans to give you hope and a future."

Jeremiah 31:3 The Lord appeared to us in the past, saying: "I have loved you with an everlasting love; I have drawn you with loving-kindness."

Isaiah 41:9–10

2. God's care and concern for his children are constant.

Deuteronomy 31:8 The Lord himself goes before you and will be with you; he will never leave you nor forsake you. Do not be afraid; do not be discouraged.

Psalm 84:11 For the Lord God is a sun and shield; the Lord bestows favor and honor; no good thing does he withhold from those whose walk is blameless.

Isaiah 40:28–31; Romans 8:38–39

3. We can enjoy contentment with self and with our situation.

Psalm 139:13–14 For you created my inmost being; you knit me together in my mother's womb. I praise you because I am fearfully and wonderfully made; your works are wonderful, I know that full well.

Philippians 4:12–13 I know what it is to be in need, and I know what it is to have plenty. I have learned the secret of being content in any and every situation, whether well fed or hungry, whether living in plenty or in want. I can do everything through him who gives me strength.

4. **Contentment is found in a close walk with God and enhanced through Christian friends.**

Psalm 17:15 And I—in righteousness I will see your face; when I awake, I will be satisfied with seeing your likeness.

Psalm 103:2–5 Praise the LORD, O my soul, and forget not all his benefits—who forgives all your sins and heals all your diseases, who redeems your life from the pit and crowns you with love and compassion, who satisfies your desires with good things so that your youth is renewed like the eagle's.

Psalm 62:5–8; 2 Corinthians 12:9; Hebrews 10:24–25

Sleeplessness

See also Fear, Worry

1. **Making godly choices during the day will help give us sweet sleep at night.**

   Proverbs 3:21–24 My son, preserve sound judgment and discernment, do not let them out of your sight; they will be life for you, an ornament to grace your neck. Then you will go on your way in safety, and your foot will not stumble; when you lie down, you will not be afraid; when you lie down, your sleep will be sweet.

   Proverbs 6:20–22 My son, keep your father's commands and do not forsake your mother's teaching. Bind them upon your heart forever; fasten them around your neck. When you walk, they will guide you; when you sleep, they will watch over you; when you awake, they will speak to you.

   Proverbs 19:23 The fear of the LORD leads to life: Then one rests content, untouched by trouble.

2. **God, who made the night, guards the night, so why should we not sleep?**

   Psalm 74:16 The day is yours, and yours also the night; you established the sun and moon.

   Psalm 121:3–4 He will not let your foot slip—he who watches over you will not slumber; indeed, he who watches over Israel will neither slumber nor sleep.

   Psalm 4:8 I will lie down and sleep in peace, for you alone, O LORD, make me dwell in safety.

   Genesis 1:3–5; Psalm 91:5; 139:11–12

3. **Prayer, coupled with carefully monitored thinking, will assist getting to sleep.**

Philippians 4:6–8 Do not be anxious about anything, but in everything, by prayer and petition, with thanksgiving, present your requests to God. And the peace of God, which transcends all understanding, will guard your hearts and your minds in Christ Jesus. Finally, brothers, whatever is true, whatever is noble, whatever is right, whatever is pure, whatever is lovely, whatever is admirable—if anything is excellent or praiseworthy—think about such things.

4. **Even though we face a variety of struggles, resting in God's sovereignty will help us sleep.**

Psalm 3:1–6 O Lord, how many are my foes! How many rise up against me! Many are saying of me, "God will not deliver him." But you are a shield around me, O Lord; you bestow glory on me and lift up my head. To the Lord I cry aloud, and he answers me from his holy hill. I lie down and sleep; I wake again, because the Lord sustains me. I will not fear the tens of thousands drawn up against me on every side.

Psalm 18:28; 92:1–2; 127:1–2; Matthew 6:33–34

5. **God can teach and instruct, even at night amid insomnia.**

Psalm 16:7–9 I will praise the Lord, who counsels me; even at night my heart instructs me. I have set the Lord always before me. Because he is at my right hand, I will not be shaken. Therefore my heart is glad and my tongue rejoices; my body also will rest secure.

Isaiah 26:9 My soul yearns for you in the night; in the morning my spirit longs for you. When your judgments come upon the earth, the people of the world learn righteousness.

6. **When sleep will not come, spend time praying and giving thanks, quoting Scripture, and singing.**

Psalm 42:8 By day the Lord directs his love, at night his song is with me—a prayer to the God of my life.

Psalm 1:2 But his delight is in the law of the Lord, and on his law he meditates day and night.

Psalm 63:6–8 On my bed I remember you; I think of you through the watches of the night. Because you are my help, I sing in the shadow of your wings. My soul clings to you; your right hand upholds me.

Psalm 77:6 I remembered my songs in the night. My heart mused and my spirit inquired.

Psalm 149:5

Biblical Illustration—God using an insomniac king to help save the Jews from destruction (Esther 6:1–3; see complete book of Esther)

Note: It could be beneficial for the counselee to see a physician.

Special Needs

See also Suffering, Health, Self-Worth

1. God takes special interest in anyone with special needs.

Psalm 82:3 Defend the cause of the weak and fatherless; maintain the rights of the poor and oppressed.

Isaiah 42:16 I will lead the blind by ways they have not known, along unfamiliar paths I will guide them; I will turn the darkness into light before them and make the rough places smooth. These are the things I will do; I will not forsake them.

1 Corinthians 1:27–29 But God chose the foolish things of the world to shame the wise; God chose the weak things of the world to shame the strong. He chose the lowly things of this world and the despised things—and the things that are not—to nullify the things that are, so that no one may boast before him.

2. We are all God's special creation, made-to-order in his image.

Psalm 139:13–16 For you created my inmost being; you knit me together in my mother's womb. I praise you because I am fearfully and wonderfully made; your works are wonderful, I know that full well. My frame was not hidden from you when I was made in the secret place. When I was woven together in the depths of the earth, your eyes saw my unformed body. All the days ordained for me were written in your book before one of them came to be.

Psalm 40:5 Many, O LORD my God, are the wonders you have done. The things you planned for us no one can recount to you; were I to speak and tell of them, they would be too many to declare.

Isaiah 44:24 This is what the Lord says—your Redeemer, who formed you in the womb: I am the Lord, who has made all things, who alone stretched out the heavens, who spread out the earth by myself.

Psalm 119:73; 2 Corinthians 4:7

3. **For purposes unknown to us, God sometimes allows accidents to happen, resulting in permanent physical or mental injury. We must trust him to help us through such difficult events, and we can find security in his love.**

Ephesians 1:11–12 In him we were also chosen, having been predestined according to the plan of him who works out everything in conformity with the purpose of his will, in order that we, who were the first to hope in Christ, might be for the praise of his glory.

1 Peter 4:12–13 Dear friends, do not be surprised at the painful trial you are suffering, as though something strange were happening to you. But rejoice that you participate in the sufferings of Christ, so that you may be overjoyed when his glory is revealed.

Psalm 138:8 The Lord will fulfill his purpose for me; your love, O Lord, endures forever—do not abandon the works of your hands.

Psalm 48:14 For this God is our God for ever and ever; he will be our guide even to the end.

Psalm 18:28; 25:4–5; Jeremiah 31:3

4. **Everyone must be treated with compassion and kindness.**

Proverbs 31:9 Speak up and judge fairly; defend the rights of the poor and needy.

Psalm 82:3–4 Defend the cause of the weak and fatherless; maintain the rights of the poor and oppressed. Rescue the weak and needy; deliver them from the hand of the wicked.

Psalm 41:1; Proverbs 14:21

5. **Provision should be made for the special needs of the handicapped.**

Leviticus 19:14 Do not curse the deaf or put a stumbling block in front of the blind, but fear your God. I am the Lord.

Luke 14:13–14 But when you give a banquet, invite the poor, the crippled, the lame, the blind, and you will be blessed. Although they cannot repay you, you will be repaid at the resurrection of the righteous.

6. God sees us as we truly are inside.

1 Samuel 16:7 But the LORD said to Samuel, "Do not consider his appearance or his height, for I have rejected him. The LORD does not look at the things man looks at. Man looks at the outward appearance, but the LORD looks at the heart."

2 Chronicles 16:9 For the eyes of the LORD range throughout the earth to strengthen those whose hearts are fully committed to him.

7. The day is coming when every believer will have a body just like Jesus.

Philippians 3:20–21 But our citizenship is in heaven. And we eagerly await a Savior from there, the Lord Jesus Christ, who, by the power that enables him to bring everything under his control, will transform our lowly bodies so that they will be like his glorious body.

2 Corinthians 5:1–4 Now we know that if the earthly tent we live in is destroyed, we have a building from God, an eternal house in heaven, not built by human hands. Meanwhile we groan, longing to be clothed with our heavenly dwelling, because when we are clothed, we will not be found naked. For while we are in this tent, we groan and are burdened, because we do not wish to be unclothed but to be clothed with our heavenly dwelling, so that what is mortal may be swallowed up by life.

1 John 3:2

Biblical Illustration—Mephibosheth (2 Samuel 9)

Speech

See also Lying, Profanity, Complaining, Words That Hurt

1. Positive qualities to develop in speech.

Building up

Ephesians 4:29 Do not let any unwholesome talk come out of your mouths, but only what is helpful for building others up according to their needs, that it may benefit those who listen.

Gentleness

Proverbs 16:24 Pleasant words are a honeycomb, sweet to the soul and healing to the bones.

Proverbs 25:15 Through patience a ruler can be persuaded, and a gentle tongue can break a bone.

Speaking truth

Ephesians 4:25 Therefore each of you must put off falsehood and speak truthfully to his neighbor, for we are all members of one body.

Speaking after listening

James 1:19–20 My dear brothers, take note of this: Everyone should be quick to listen, slow to speak and slow to become angry, for man's anger does not bring about the righteous life that God desires.

Proverbs 15:28 The heart of the righteous weighs its answers, but the mouth of the wicked gushes evil.

Communicating knowledge

Proverbs 20:15 Gold there is, and rubies in abundance, but lips that speak knowledge are a rare jewel.

Appropriate words

Proverbs 25:11 A word aptly spoken is like apples of gold in settings of silver.

Proverbs 15:23 A man finds joy in giving an apt reply—and how good is a timely word!

Kindness

Proverbs 12:25 An anxious heart weighs a man down, but a kind word cheers him up.

Ephesians 4:32 Be kind and compassionate to one another, forgiving each other, just as in Christ God forgave you.

2. Negative qualities to avoid in speech.

Obscene, foolish, raw jokes

Ephesians 5:4 Nor should there be obscenity, foolish talk or coarse joking, which are out of place, but rather thanksgiving.

Ephesians 4:29 Do not let any unwholesome talk come out of your mouths, but only what is helpful for building others up according to their needs, that it may benefit those who listen.

Falsehood, lying

Ephesians 4:25 Therefore each of you must put off falsehood and speak truthfully to his neighbor, for we are all members of one body.

Answering before listening

Proverbs 18:13 He who answers before listening—that is his folly and his shame.

Foolish, stupid arguments

2 Timothy 2:23–24 Don't have anything to do with foolish and stupid arguments, because you know they produce quarrels. And the

Lord's servant must not quarrel; instead, he must be kind to everyone, able to teach, not resentful.

Slander

Titus 3:1–2 Remind the people to be subject to rulers and authorities, to be obedient, to be ready to do whatever is good, to slander no one, to be peaceable and considerate, and to show true humility toward all men.

Lack of control

James 1:26 If anyone considers himself religious and yet does not keep a tight rein on his tongue, he deceives himself and his religion is worthless.

3. Speech can both grieve and please the Holy Spirit.

Ephesians 4:29–31 Do not let any unwholesome talk come out of your mouths, but only what is helpful for building others up according to their needs, that it may benefit those who listen. And do not grieve the Holy Spirit of God, with whom you were sealed for the day of redemption. Get rid of all bitterness, rage and anger, brawling and slander, along with every form of malice.

4. Summary of the tongue's power potential.

Proverbs 18:21 The tongue has the power of life and death, and those who love it will eat its fruit.

James 3:5–8 Likewise the tongue is a small part of the body, but it makes great boasts. Consider what a great forest is set on fire by a small spark. The tongue also is a fire, a world of evil among the parts of the body. It corrupts the whole person, sets the whole course of his life on fire, and is itself set on fire by hell. All kinds of animals, birds, reptiles and creatures of the sea are being tamed and have been tamed by man, but no man can tame the tongue. It is a restless evil, full of deadly poison.

James 3:9–12

5. Many contrasts are provided in Proverbs.

Proverbs 12:18 Reckless words pierce like a sword, but the tongue of the wise brings healing.

Proverbs 15:1 A gentle answer turns away wrath, but a harsh word stirs up anger.

Proverbs 15:4 The tongue that brings healing is a tree of life, but a deceitful tongue crushes the spirit.

Proverbs 10:20–21

Biblical Illustration—Abigail (1 Samuel 25)

Spiritual Gifts

See also Church Life

1. Every believer has at least one spiritual gift.

1 Corinthians 12:4–7, 11 There are different kinds of gifts, but the same Spirit. There are different kinds of service, but the same Lord. There are different kinds of working, but the same God works all of them in all men. Now to each one the manifestation of the Spirit is given for the common good.... All these are the work of one and the same Spirit, and he gives them to each one, just as he determines.

Ephesians 4:7–8 But to each one of us grace has been given as Christ apportioned it. This is why it says: "When he ascended on high, he led captives in his train and gave gifts to men."

2. We need to know what spiritual gifts are available and how to use them to be able to effectively serve in the body of Christ.

1 Peter 4:10–11 Each one should use whatever gift he has received to serve others, faithfully administering God's grace in its various forms. If anyone speaks, he should do it as one speaking the very words of God. If anyone serves, he should do it with the strength God provides, so that in all things God may be praised through Jesus Christ. To him be the glory and the power for ever and ever. Amen.

Romans 12:6–8 We have different gifts, according to the grace given us. If a man's gift is prophesying, let him use it in proportion to his faith. If it is serving, let him serve; if it is teaching, let him teach; if it is encouraging, let him encourage; if it is contributing to the needs of others, let him give generously; if it is leadership, let him govern diligently; if it is showing mercy, let him do it cheerfully.

Note: Youth workers should provide guidance to enable their young people to discover and use individual spiritual gifts.

Spiritual Warfare

Occult/Psychics/Astrology/Satan

See also Choices, Temptation

1. Satan is a liar and murderer, our enemy who seeks our destruction.

John 8:44 You belong to your father, the devil, and you want to carry out your father's desire. He was a murderer from the beginning, not holding to the truth, for there is no truth in him. When he lies, he speaks his native language, for he is a liar and the father of lies.

1 Peter 5:8 Be self-controlled and alert. Your enemy the devil prowls around like a roaring lion looking for someone to devour.

2. Satan attempts to deceive us with his counterfeits.

Isaiah 14:13–14 You said in your heart, "I will ascend to heaven; I will raise my throne above the stars of God; I will sit enthroned on the mount of assembly, on the utmost heights of the sacred mountain. I will ascend above the tops of the clouds; I will make myself like the Most High."

2 Corinthians 11:14 And no wonder, for Satan himself masquerades as an angel of light.

1 John 4:1 Dear friends, do not believe every spirit, but test the spirits to see whether they are from God, because many false prophets have gone out into the world.

Deuteronomy 13:1–3; 1 Timothy 4:1

3. **Satan uses demons in his schemes to defeat Christians and to keep people from coming to Christ.**

Ephesians 6:11–12 Put on the full armor of God so that you can take your stand against the devil's schemes. For our struggle is not against flesh and blood, but against the rulers, against the authorities, against the powers of this dark world and against the spiritual forces of evil in the heavenly realms.

Revelation 12:9 The great dragon was hurled down—that ancient serpent called the devil, or Satan, who leads the whole world astray. He was hurled to the earth, and his angels with him.

Ephesians 2:1–2

4. **God forbids any involvement with satanic practices, occult mediums, or beliefs, including games, movies, and reading materials that have pro-satanic content.**

Deuteronomy 18:10–12 Let no one be found among you who sacrifices his son or daughter in the fire, who practices divination or sorcery, interprets omens, engages in witchcraft, or casts spells, or who is a medium or spiritist or who consults the dead. Anyone who does these things is detestable to the LORD.

Isaiah 8:19 When men tell you to consult mediums and spiritists, who whisper and mutter, should not a people inquire of their God? Why consult the dead on behalf of the living?

Galatians 5:19–21

5. **God, not astrology, is in control of the events of our lives.**

Jeremiah 10:2 This is what the LORD says: "Do not learn the ways of the nations or be terrified by signs in the sky, though the nations are terrified by them."

Isaiah 47:13–14 All the counsel you have received has only worn you out! Let your astrologers come forward, those stargazers who make predictions month by month, let them save you from what is coming upon you. Surely they are like stubble; the fire will burn them up. They cannot even save themselves from the power of the flame. Here are no coals to warm anyone; here is no fire to sit by.

Daniel 4:35 All the peoples of the earth are regarded as nothing. He does as he pleases with the powers of heaven and the peoples of the earth. No one can hold back his hand or say to him: "What have you done?"

Deuteronomy 4:19; Job 42:1–2

6. **The heavenly bodies (stars, planets, sun, and moon) were created by God to light the world and express God's glory, not to reveal or guide us to our destiny.**

Genesis 1:16–18 God made two great lights—the greater light to govern the day and the lesser light to govern the night. He also made the stars. God set them in the expanse of the sky to give light on the earth, to govern the day and the night, and to separate light from darkness. And God saw that it was good.

Isaiah 40:26 Lift your eyes and look to the heavens: Who created all these? He who brings out the starry host one by one, and calls them each by name. Because of his great power and mighty strength, not one of them is missing.

Psalm 19:1; 108:4–5

7. **Reincarnation is not taught in Scripture.**

Genesis 3:19 By the sweat of your brow you will eat your food until you return to the ground, since from it you were taken; for dust you are and to dust you will return.

Hebrews 9:27 Just as man is destined to die once, and after that to face judgment.

8. **Be on guard, and depend on God's power to stand strong against Satan.**

2 Thessalonians 3:3 But the Lord is faithful, and he will strengthen and protect you from the evil one.

James 4:7 Submit yourselves, then, to God. Resist the devil, and he will flee from you.

Ephesians 4:27 And do not give the devil a foothold.

Ephesians 6:10–18; 1 Peter 5:8

211

9. Destroy all items related to the occult and its practices.

Acts 19:18–20 Many of those who believed now came and openly confessed their evil deeds. A number who had practiced sorcery brought their scrolls together and burned them publicly. When they calculated the value of the scrolls, the total came to fifty thousand drachmas. In this way the word of the Lord spread widely and grew in power.

James 1:21 Therefore, get rid of all moral filth and the evil that is so prevalent and humbly accept the word planted in you, which can save you.

2 Corinthians 6:14–17

Biblical Illustrations—Jesus and demonic activity (Mark 5:1–20, among other Scriptures); Simon the magician (Acts 8:9–24); slave girl (Acts 16:16–18)

Sports/Exercise

See also Cheating, Integrity, Pride

1. **Taking care of our physical bodies is one way to honor the Holy Spirit, who lives inside of us.**

    1 Corinthians 6:19–20 Do you not know that your body is a temple of the Holy Spirit, who is in you, whom you have received from God? You are not your own; you were bought at a price. Therefore honor God with your body.

    Psalm 139:13–16 For you created my inmost being; you knit me together in my mother's womb. I praise you because I am fearfully and wonderfully made; your works are wonderful, I know that full well. My frame was not hidden from you when I was made in the secret place. When I was woven together in the depths of the earth, your eyes saw my unformed body.

2. **Cheating is stealing if you take a prize that belongs to another.**

    2 Timothy 2:5 Similarly, if anyone competes as an athlete, he does not receive the victor's crown unless he competes according to the rules.

    Exodus 20:15 You shall not steal.

    Ephesians 4:28 He who has been stealing must steal no longer, but must work, doing something useful with his own hands, that he may have something to share with those in need.

    Ephesians 4:25

3. **It takes great effort and sacrifice to win the prize.**

    1 Corinthians 9:24–25 Do you not know that in a race all the runners run, but only one gets the prize? Run in such a way as to get the prize. Everyone who competes in the games goes into strict training. They do it to get a crown that will not last; but we do it to get a crown that will last forever.

1 Corinthians 9:26–27

4. **Doing what God wants is much more valuable than winning an earthly prize or having a buff body.**

1 Timothy 4:8 For physical training is of some value, but godliness has value for all things, holding promise for both the present life and the life to come.

Philippians 3:14 I press on toward the goal to win the prize for which God has called me heavenward in Christ Jesus.

1 Timothy 6:12 Fight the good fight of the faith. Take hold of the eternal life to which you were called when you made your good confession in the presence of many witnesses.

Hebrews 12:1–2; James 1:12

Stealing/Cheating

See also Lying, Integrity, Choices

1. **Taking something that does not belong to you is always wrong.**

   Exodus 20:15 You shall not steal.

   Proverbs 28:24 He who robs his father or mother and says, "It's not wrong"—he is partner to him who destroys.

2. **It is cheating and stealing when you take a prize, an award, or a grade that belongs to someone else. It is lying when you say that what you have done is your own accomplishment when it is not.**

   Leviticus 19:11–12 Do not steal. Do not lie. Do not deceive one another. Do not swear falsely by my name and so profane the name of your God. I am the LORD.

3. **As with any sin, God requires repentance and confession.**

   1 John 1:6–10 If we claim to have fellowship with him yet walk in the darkness, we lie and do not live by the truth. But if we walk in the light, as he is in the light, we have fellowship with one another, and the blood of Jesus, his Son, purifies us from all sin. If we claim to be without sin, we deceive ourselves and the truth is not in us. If we confess our sins, he is faithful and just and will forgive us our sins and purify us from all unrighteousness. If we claim we have not sinned, we make him out to be a liar and his word has no place in our lives.

4. **A change in thinking and lifestyle is needed.**

   Romans 13:9 The commandments, "Do not commit adultery," "Do not murder," "Do not steal," "Do not covet," and whatever other commandment there may be, are summed up in this one rule: "Love your neighbor as yourself."

Ephesians 4:28 He who has been stealing must steal no longer, but must work, doing something useful with his own hands, that he may have something to share with those in need.

5. Restitution is required.

Leviticus 6:2–5 If anyone sins and is unfaithful to the Lord by deceiving his neighbor about something entrusted to him or left in his care or stolen, or if he cheats him, or if he finds lost property and lies about it, or if he swears falsely, or if he commits any such sin that people may do—when he thus sins and becomes guilty, he must return what he has stolen or taken by extortion, or what was entrusted to him, or the lost property he found, or whatever it was he swore falsely about.

Biblical Illustration—Achan (Joshua 7)

Suffering/Adversity

See also Natural Disasters, Fear, Health

1. **Because we live in a fallen world, going through difficult times is inevitable.**

   Job 5:7 Yet man is born to trouble as surely as sparks fly upward.

   John 16:33 I have told you these things, so that in me you may have peace. In this world you will have trouble. But take heart! I have overcome the world.

   Romans 8:18–23; 1 Peter 4:12

Purpose for Adversity

1. **It makes our faith stronger.**

   1 Peter 1:6–7 In this you greatly rejoice, though now for a little while you may have had to suffer grief in all kinds of trials. These have come so that your faith—of greater worth than gold, which perishes even though refined by fire—may be proved genuine and may result in praise, glory and honor when Jesus Christ is revealed.

2. **It helps us grow into the kind of people God wants us to be.**

   Job 23:8–10 But if I go to the east, he is not there; if I go to the west, I do not find him. When he is at work in the north, I do not see him; when he turns to the south, I catch no glimpse of him. But he knows the way that I take; when he has tested me, I will come forth as gold.

   Philippians 3:7–8; James 1:2–4

3. It causes us to think more about heaven and eternity.

2 Corinthians 4:16–18 Therefore we do not lose heart. Though outwardly we are wasting away, yet inwardly we are being renewed day by day. For our light and momentary troubles are achieving for us an eternal glory that far outweighs them all. So we fix our eyes not on what is seen, but on what is unseen. For what is seen is temporary, but what is unseen is eternal.

4. It disciplines us for our sins.

Hebrews 12:10–11 Our fathers disciplined us for a little while as they thought best; but God disciplines us for our good, that we may share in his holiness. No discipline seems pleasant at the time, but painful. Later on, however, it produces a harvest of righteousness and peace for those who have been trained by it.

Proverbs 3:11–12

What Our Response Should Be

1. Realize God's grace is sufficient.

Psalm 55:22 Cast your cares on the LORD and he will sustain you; he will never let the righteous fall.

2 Corinthians 12:9 But he said to me, "My grace is sufficient for you, for my power is made perfect in weakness." Therefore I will boast all the more gladly about my weaknesses, so that Christ's power may rest on me.

2. Remember God is sovereign even in adversity.

Psalm 71:20–21 Though you have made me see troubles, many and bitter, you will restore my life again; from the depths of the earth you will again bring me up. You will increase my honor and comfort me once again.

Psalm 33:13–15; Isaiah 43:1–2

3. Know that God is there to listen and respond.

Psalm 9:9–10 The LORD is a refuge for the oppressed, a stronghold in times of trouble. Those who know your name will trust in you, for you, LORD, have never forsaken those who seek you.

Psalm 31:9–10 Be merciful to me, O Lord, for I am in distress; my eyes grow weak with sorrow, my soul and my body with grief. My life is consumed by anguish and my years by groaning; my strength fails because of my affliction, and my bones grow weak.

Psalm 61:2 From the ends of the earth I call to you, I call as my heart grows faint; lead me to the rock that is higher than I.

Psalm 3:4; 86:3

4. Use the help God gives us to help others.

2 Corinthians 1:3–4 Praise be to the God and Father of our Lord Jesus Christ, the Father of compassion and the God of all comfort, who comforts us in all our troubles, so that we can comfort those in any trouble with the comfort we ourselves have received from God.

5. Know that adversity results in God's reward.

James 1:12 Blessed is the man who perseveres under trial, because when he has stood the test, he will receive the crown of life that God has promised to those who love him.

1 Peter 5:10 And the God of all grace, who called you to his eternal glory in Christ, after you have suffered a little while, will himself restore you and make you strong, firm and steadfast.

Biblical Illustrations—Job; Joseph (Genesis narratives); Stephen (Acts 7); Paul and Silas (Acts 16)

Suicide

See also Depression, Fear, Self-Worth, Loneliness

1. **We belong to God; we are his. Therefore, ending our life is not an option.**

    Psalm 139:13–16 For you created my inmost being; you knit me together in my mother's womb. I praise you because I am fearfully and wonderfully made; your works are wonderful, I know that full well. My frame was not hidden from you when I was made in the secret place. When I was woven together in the depths of the earth, your eyes saw my unformed body. All the days ordained for me were written in your book before one of them came to be.

    1 Corinthians 6:19–20 Do you not know that your body is a temple of the Holy Spirit, who is in you, whom you have received from God? You are not your own; you were bought at a price. Therefore honor God with your body.

2. **God sending his Son to die for us shows how much he loves us.**

    Romans 5:8 But God demonstrates his own love for us in this: While we were still sinners, Christ died for us.

    Ephesians 2:4–5 But because of his great love for us, God, who is rich in mercy, made us alive with Christ even when we were dead in transgressions—it is by grace you have been saved.

    John 3:16; 1 Peter 2:9

3. **If someone is contemplating suicide because of some terrible sin committed, he or she needs to realize that there is no sin too great for God to forgive.**

Micah 7:18–19 Who is a God like you, who pardons sin and forgives the transgression of the remnant of his inheritance? You do not stay angry forever but delight to show mercy. You will again have compassion on us; you will tread our sins underfoot and hurl all our iniquities into the depths of the sea.

Isaiah 43:25 I, even I, am he who blots out your transgressions, for my own sake, and remembers your sins no more.

Psalm 145:8; 1 John 1:9

4. **God is with us even in the darkest of times.**

Psalm 139:7–12 Where can I go from your Spirit? Where can I flee from your presence? If I go up to the heavens, you are there; if I make my bed in the depths, you are there. If I rise on the wings of the dawn, if I settle on the far side of the sea, even there your hand will guide me, your right hand will hold me fast. If I say, "Surely the darkness will hide me and the light become night around me," even the darkness will not be dark to you; the night will shine like the day, for darkness is as light to you.

5. **There is no problem too great for God to handle.**

Jeremiah 32:17 Ah, Sovereign LORD, you have made the heavens and the earth by your great power and outstretched arm. Nothing is too hard for you.

Isaiah 43:18–19 Forget the former things; do not dwell on the past. See, I am doing a new thing! Now it springs up; do you not perceive it? I am making a way in the desert and streams in the wasteland.

Isaiah 41:10; Jeremiah 33:3

6. **Our future is secure with God on our side.**

Jeremiah 29:11–13 "For I know the plans I have for you," declares the LORD, "plans to prosper you and not to harm you, plans to give you hope and a future. Then you will call upon me and come and pray to me, and I will listen to you. You will seek me and find me when you seek me with all your heart."

Romans 8:38–39 For I am convinced that neither death nor life, neither angels nor demons, neither the present nor the future, nor any powers, neither height nor depth, nor anything else in all creation, will be able to separate us from the love of God that is in Christ Jesus our Lord.

7. God will never leave us.

Deuteronomy 31:8 The LORD himself goes before you and will be with you; he will never leave you nor forsake you. Do not be afraid; do not be discouraged.

Joshua 1:9 Have I not commanded you? Be strong and courageous. Do not be terrified; do not be discouraged, for the LORD your God will be with you wherever you go.

8. We must immerse ourselves in the Word of God, letting it saturate our very being.

Joshua 1:8 Do not let this Book of the Law depart from your mouth; meditate on it day and night, so that you may be careful to do everything written in it. Then you will be prosperous and successful.

Psalm 119:105 Your word is a lamp to my feet and a light for my path.

Hebrews 4:12

9. If suicide does occur, God's grace extends even to that sin. A Christian who takes his or her own life will still go to heaven.

John 10:27–29 My sheep listen to my voice; I know them, and they follow me. I give them eternal life, and they shall never perish; no one can snatch them out of my hand. My Father, who has given them to me, is greater than all; no one can snatch them out of my Father's hand.

Romans 8:38–39 For I am convinced that neither death nor life, neither angels nor demons, neither the present nor the future, nor any powers, neither height nor depth, nor anything else in all creation, will be able to separate us from the love of God that is in Christ Jesus our Lord.

Hebrews 7:25

Note: It would be beneficial to have the counselee see a physician, pastor, or trained biblical counselor.

Temptation

See also Choices

1. Temptation is not sin but comes as a result of our sinful nature.

James 1:14 But each one is tempted when, by his own evil desire, he is dragged away and enticed.

Romans 7:18 I know that nothing good lives in me, that is, in my sinful nature. For I have the desire to do what is good, but I cannot carry it out.

1 Corinthians 10:13

2. Though Christ never sinned, he understands our temptations and is able to help us in them.

Hebrews 2:18 Because he himself suffered when he was tempted, he is able to help those who are being tempted.

Hebrews 4:15 For we do not have a high priest who is unable to sympathize with our weaknesses, but we have one who has been tempted in every way, just as we are—yet was without sin.

3. Asking God for help to avoid and handle temptation is vital.

Psalm 19:13 Keep your servant also from willful sins; may they not rule over me. Then will I be blameless, innocent of great transgression.

James 4:7 Submit yourselves, then, to God. Resist the devil, and he will flee from you.

Luke 11:4; Hebrews 4:16

4. **Seeking out other strong believers for accountability and support is necessary.**

Galatians 6:2 Carry each other's burdens, and in this way you will fulfill the law of Christ.

Romans 15:1 We who are strong ought to bear with the failings of the weak and not to please ourselves.

James 5:16 Therefore confess your sins to each other and pray for each other so that you may be healed. The prayer of a righteous man is powerful and effective.

5. **Choosing to serve God rather than sin is crucial in resisting temptation.**

Joshua 24:14–15 Now fear the LORD and serve him with all faithfulness. Throw away the gods your forefathers worshiped beyond the River and in Egypt, and serve the LORD. But if serving the LORD seems undesirable to you, then choose for yourselves this day whom you will serve, whether the gods your forefathers served beyond the River, or the gods of the Amorites, in whose land you are living. But as for me and my household, we will serve the LORD.

Psalm 37:27 Turn from evil and do good; then you will dwell in the land forever.

6. **Christ's death included provision for victory over sin.**

Romans 6:6, 11–13 For we know that our old self was crucified with him so that the body of sin might be done away with, that we should no longer be slaves to sin. . . . In the same way, count yourselves dead to sin but alive to God in Christ Jesus. Therefore do not let sin reign in your mortal body so that you obey its evil desires. Do not offer the parts of your body to sin, as instruments of wickedness, but rather offer yourselves to God, as those who have been brought from death to life; and offer the parts of your body to him as instruments of righteousness.

[Note the "know," "count," "offer" sequence for action steps.]

2 Peter 1:3 His divine power has given us everything we need for life and godliness through our knowledge of him who called us by his own glory and goodness.

7. **It takes courage and God's help to stand up against temptation.**

Ephesians 6:10–11 Finally, be strong in the Lord and in his mighty power. Put on the full armor of God so that you can take your stand against the devil's schemes.

Hebrews 12:1–2 Therefore, since we are surrounded by such a great cloud of witnesses, let us throw off everything that hinders and the sin that so easily entangles, and let us run with perseverance the race marked out for us. Let us fix our eyes on Jesus, the author and perfecter of our faith, who for the joy set before him endured the cross, scorning its shame, and sat down at the right hand of the throne of God.

1 John 4:4 You, dear children, are from God and have overcome them, because the one who is in you is greater than the one who is in the world.

Proverbs 4:14–15; Ephesians 6:12–18; James 1:12

8. **Saying no to temptation may require paying a high price, but doing so is worth the cost.**

Matthew 5:10–12 Blessed are those who are persecuted because of righteousness, for theirs is the kingdom of heaven. Blessed are you when people insult you, persecute you and falsely say all kinds of evil against you because of me. Rejoice and be glad, because great is your reward in heaven.

1 Peter 4:14 If you are insulted because of the name of Christ, you are blessed, for the Spirit of glory and of God rests on you.

Hebrews 11:24–25

9. **Be careful in helping others flee temptation; do not be caught yourself.**

Galatians 6:1 Brothers, if someone is caught in a sin, you who are spiritual should restore him gently. But watch yourself, or you also may be tempted.

1 Peter 5:8–9 Be self-controlled and alert. Your enemy the devil prowls around like a roaring lion looking for someone to devour. Resist him, standing firm in the faith, because you know that your brothers throughout the world are undergoing the same kind of sufferings.

1 Timothy 6:9–10

Biblical Illustration—Joseph (Genesis 39)

Thought Life/Fantasizing

See also Lust, Sexual Purity, Mind, Pornography

1. We must discipline ourselves to have right thinking.

1 Peter 1:13 Therefore, prepare your minds for action; be self-controlled; set your hope fully on the grace to be given you when Jesus Christ is revealed.

Philippians 4:8 Finally, brothers, whatever is true, whatever is noble, whatever is right, whatever is pure, whatever is lovely, whatever is admirable—if anything is excellent or praiseworthy—think about such things.

2 Corinthians 10:5 We demolish arguments and every pretension that sets itself up against the knowledge of God, and we take captive every thought to make it obedient to Christ.

2. No thought or secret place is hidden from God.

Psalm 139:1–4 O Lord, you have searched me and you know me. You know when I sit and when I rise; you perceive my thoughts from afar. You discern my going out and my lying down; you are familiar with all my ways. Before a word is on my tongue you know it completely, O LORD.

Jeremiah 23:23–24 "Am I only a God nearby," declares the LORD, "and not a God far away? Can anyone hide in secret places so that I cannot see him?" declares the LORD. "Do not I fill heaven and earth?" declares the LORD.

Hebrews 4:13 Nothing in all creation is hidden from God's sight. Everything is uncovered and laid bare before the eyes of him to whom we must give account.

2 Chronicles 16:9

3. **Thinking as God thinks should be our standard. Put evil thoughts aside.**

Isaiah 55:7–8 Let the wicked forsake his way and the evil man his thoughts. Let him turn to the LORD, and he will have mercy on him, and to our God, for he will freely pardon. "For my thoughts are not your thoughts, neither are your ways my ways," declares the LORD.

Ephesians 4:22–24 You were taught, with regard to your former way of life, to put off your old self, which is being corrupted by its deceitful desires; to be made new in the attitude of your minds; and to put on the new self, created to be like God in true righteousness and holiness.

Romans 12:2

4. **Lustful thoughts are sinful and must be avoided.**

Matthew 5:28 But I tell you that anyone who looks at a woman lustfully has already committed adultery with her in his heart.

Job 31:1 I made a covenant with my eyes not to look lustfully at a girl.

1 Thessalonians 4:3–5

Time Management

See also Laziness, Work Ethic

1. Skills for personal time management must be developed early in life.

Psalm 39:4–5 Show me, O LORD, my life's end and the number of my days; let me know how fleeting is my life. You have made my days a mere handbreadth; the span of my years is as nothing before you. Each man's life is but a breath.

Psalm 90:12 Teach us to number our days aright, that we may gain a heart of wisdom.

Ephesians 5:15–17 Be very careful, then, how you live—not as unwise but as wise, making the most of every opportunity, because the days are evil. Therefore do not be foolish, but understand what the Lord's will is.

2. Depending on God for all our plans is essential.

Psalm 90:17 May the favor of the Lord our God rest upon us; establish the work of our hands for us—yes, establish the work of our hands.

Proverbs 3:5–6 Trust in the LORD with all your heart and lean not on your own understanding; in all your ways acknowledge him, and he will make your paths straight.

James 4:13–15 Now listen, you who say, "Today or tomorrow we will go to this or that city, spend a year there, carry on business and make money." Why, you do not even know what will happen tomorrow. What is your life? You are a mist that appears for a little while and then vanishes. Instead, you ought to say, "If it is the Lord's will, we will live and do this or that."

3. We need to pray for wisdom regarding all our plans.

James 1:5 If any of you lacks wisdom, he should ask God, who gives generously to all without finding fault, and it will be given to him.

Proverbs 2:6–9 For the LORD gives wisdom, and from his mouth come knowledge and understanding. He holds victory in store for the upright, he is a shield to those whose walk is blameless, for he guards the course of the just and protects the way of his faithful ones. Then you will understand what is right and just and fair—every good path.

Trust/Faith

See also Suffering, Fear

1. Faith brings certainty and reality to that which is otherwise unknown.

Hebrews 11:1 Now faith is being sure of what we hope for and certain of what we do not see.

2. Faith is necessary to please God.

Hebrews 11:6 And without faith it is impossible to please God, because anyone who comes to him must believe that he exists and that he rewards those who earnestly seek him.

3. Trusting God for the unknown is an indication of faith.

Hebrews 11:8–9 By faith Abraham, when called to go to a place he would later receive as his inheritance, obeyed and went, even though he did not know where he was going. By faith he made his home in the promised land like a stranger in a foreign country; he lived in tents, as did Isaac and Jacob, who were heirs with him of the same promise.

Matthew 17:20 He replied, "Because you have so little faith. I tell you the truth, if you have faith as small as a mustard seed, you can say to this mountain, 'Move from here to there' and it will move. Nothing will be impossible for you."

2 Corinthians 5:7

4. We are to place our trust ultimately in God alone (although God does use other people for our benefit).

Psalm 118:8–9 It is better to take refuge in the LORD than to trust in man. It is better to take refuge in the LORD than to trust in princes.

Psalm 20:7 Some trust in chariots and some in horses, but we trust in the name of the LORD our God.

Psalm 40:4 Blessed is the man who makes the LORD his trust, who does not look to the proud, to those who turn aside to false gods.

Jeremiah 17:5–8

5. Faith can overcome physical limitations.

Hebrews 11:11–12 By faith Abraham, even though he was past age—and Sarah herself was barren—was enabled to become a father because he considered him faithful who had made the promise. And so from this one man, and he as good as dead, came descendants as numerous as the stars in the sky and as countless as the sand on the seashore.

6. Through faith we depend on God in difficult times.

Job 23:8–10 But if I go to the east, he is not there; if I go to the west, I do not find him. When he is at work in the north, I do not see him; when he turns to the south, I catch no glimpse of him. But he knows the way that I take; when he has tested me, I will come forth as gold.

Habakkuk 3:17–18 Though the fig tree does not bud and there are no grapes on the vines, though the olive crop fails and the fields produce no food, though there are no sheep in the pen and no cattle in the stalls, yet I will rejoice in the LORD, I will be joyful in God my Savior.

Job 2:10

7. Trusting God shows confidence that his timing is perfect.

Habakkuk 2:3–4 For the revelation awaits an appointed time; it speaks of the end and will not prove false. Though it linger, wait for it; it will certainly come and will not delay. See, he is puffed up; his desires are not upright—but the righteous will live by his faith.

Psalm 27:14 Wait for the LORD; be strong and take heart and wait for the LORD.

Psalm 130:5–6

8. Results of trusting God.

Protection

Psalm 5:11 But let all who take refuge in you be glad; let them ever sing for joy. Spread your protection over them, that those who love your name may rejoice in you.

Psalm 36:7 How priceless is your unfailing love! Both high and low among men find refuge in the shadow of your wings.

Proverbs 30:5

Gladness

Psalm 64:10 Let the righteous rejoice in the LORD and take refuge in him; let all the upright in heart praise him!

Peace

Isaiah 26:3–4 You will keep in perfect peace him whose mind is steadfast, because he trusts in you. Trust in the LORD forever, for the LORD, the LORD, is the Rock eternal.

Isaiah 12:2

Blessing

Psalm 84:12 O LORD Almighty, blessed is the man who trusts in you.

Jeremiah 17:7 But blessed is the man who trusts in the LORD, whose confidence is in him.

Psalm 34:8

Confidence

Psalm 112:7 He will have no fear of bad news; his heart is steadfast, trusting in the LORD.

Psalm 56:4 In God, whose word I praise, in God I trust; I will not be afraid. What can mortal man do to me?

Biblical Illustrations—Abraham (Genesis 17:15–19); three young men (Daniel 3); centurion (Matthew 8:5–10); Peter (Matthew 14:24–32)

Unwed Pregnancy

See also Abortion, Adoption, Confession

1. **Seek God's wisdom and counsel to know if the baby should be kept or given up for adoption.**

    Proverbs 2:6–12 For the LORD gives wisdom, and from his mouth come knowledge and understanding. He holds victory in store for the upright, he is a shield to those whose walk is blameless, for he guards the course of the just and protects the way of his faithful ones. Then you will understand what is right and just and fair—every good path. For wisdom will enter your heart, and knowledge will be pleasant to your soul. Discretion will protect you, and understanding will guard you. Wisdom will save you from the ways of wicked men, from men whose words are perverse.

    Psalm 139:23–24; James 1:5

2. **Go to parents and Christian leaders for help.**

    Proverbs 6:20–22 My son, keep your father's commands and do not forsake your mother's teaching. Bind them upon your heart forever; fasten them around your neck. When you walk, they will guide you; when you sleep, they will watch over you; when you awake, they will speak to you.

    Proverbs 15:22 Plans fail for lack of counsel, but with many advisers they succeed.

    Deuteronomy 5:16; Ephesians 6:1–2

3. **Each life is significant. Abortion is not an option.**

    Psalm 127:3 Sons are a heritage from the LORD, children a reward from him.

James 4:17 Anyone, then, who knows the good he ought to do and doesn't do it, sins.

4. **If this pregnancy is the result of sin (i.e., consensual intercourse), confession must be made to God and parents.**

Proverbs 28:13 He who conceals his sins does not prosper, but whoever confesses and renounces them finds mercy.

Psalm 32:5 Then I acknowledged my sin to you and did not cover up my iniquity. I said, "I will confess my transgressions to the LORD"—and you forgave the guilt of my sin.

1 John 1:8–9 If we claim to be without sin, we deceive ourselves and the truth is not in us. If we confess our sins, he is faithful and just and will forgive us our sins and purify us from all unrighteousness.

Psalm 51:1–2

5. **Find others who are godly to help bear the burden.**

Galatians 6:1–2 Brothers, if someone is caught in a sin, you who are spiritual should restore him gently. But watch yourself, or you also may be tempted. Carry each other's burdens, and in this way you will fulfill the law of Christ.

Romans 15:1 We who are strong ought to bear with the failings of the weak and not to please ourselves.

6. **God will meet your needs through these difficult days. Run to him for help.**

Psalm 46:1 God is our refuge and strength, an ever-present help in trouble.

Psalm 91:1–2 He who dwells in the shelter of the Most High will rest in the shadow of the Almighty. I will say of the LORD, "He is my refuge and my fortress, my God, in whom I trust."

Philippians 4:19 And my God will meet all your needs according to his glorious riches in Christ Jesus.

Note: It would be beneficial to have the counselee see a physician.

Words That Hurt

Gossip/Rumors/Teasing

See also Lying, Speech

1. **Words used inappropriately can bring hurt, even destruction, into the lives of all involved.**

   Leviticus 19:16 Do not go about spreading slander among your people. Do not do anything that endangers your neighbor's life. I am the LORD.

   Proverbs 16:28 A perverse man stirs up dissension, and a gossip separates close friends.

   Proverbs 26:20–22 Without wood a fire goes out; without gossip a quarrel dies down. As charcoal to embers and as wood to fire, so is a quarrelsome man for kindling strife. The words of a gossip are like choice morsels; they go down to a man's inmost parts.

   Matthew 12:35–36 The good man brings good things out of the good stored up in him, and the evil man brings evil things out of the evil stored up in him. But I tell you that men will have to give account on the day of judgment for every careless word they have spoken.

   Proverbs 11:13; 13:3; 18:21; Galatians 5:15; James 3:5–12

2. **Words used inappropriately will damage our daily walk with God.**

   Psalm 15:1–3 Lord, who may dwell in your sanctuary? Who may live on your holy hill? He whose walk is blameless and who does what is righteous, who speaks the truth from his heart and has no slander on his tongue, who does his neighbor no wrong and casts no slur on his fellowman.

2 Timothy 2:16 Avoid godless chatter, because those who indulge in it will become more and more ungodly.

3. We must choose not to use hurtful words.

Psalm 17:3 Though you probe my heart and examine me at night, though you test me, you will find nothing; I have resolved that my mouth will not sin.

Psalm 141:3 Set a guard over my mouth, O Lord; keep watch over the door of my lips.

1 Peter 3:8–10 Finally, all of you, live in harmony with one another; be sympathetic, love as brothers, be compassionate and humble. Do not repay evil with evil or insult with insult, but with blessing, because to this you were called so that you may inherit a blessing. For, "Whoever would love life and see good days must keep his tongue from evil and his lips from deceitful speech."

Proverbs 4:24; James 1:26; 1 Peter 2:1

4. Damaging words must be replaced with positive, productive words.

Proverbs 12:18 Reckless words pierce like a sword, but the tongue of the wise brings healing.

Ephesians 4:29 Do not let any unwholesome talk come out of your mouths, but only what is helpful for building others up according to their needs, that it may benefit those who listen.

Proverbs 16:24

5. God is our refuge against hurtful words.

Psalm 31:19–20 How great is your goodness, which you have stored up for those who fear you, which you bestow in the sight of men on those who take refuge in you. In the shelter of your presence you hide them from the intrigues of men; in your dwelling you keep them safe from accusing tongues.

Luke 6:22 Blessed are you when men hate you, when they exclude you and insult you and reject your name as evil, because of the Son of Man.

Psalm 62:5–7; 140:12

6. What to do when words hurt us.

Psalm 64:2–3 Hide me from the conspiracy of the wicked, from that noisy crowd of evildoers. They sharpen their tongues like swords and aim their words like deadly arrows.

Psalm 119:69 Though the arrogant have smeared me with lies, I keep your precepts with all my heart.

Psalm 120:1–2 I call on the LORD in my distress, and he answers me. Save me, O LORD, from lying lips and from deceitful tongues.

Proverbs 12:16 A fool shows his annoyance at once, but a prudent man overlooks an insult.

Luke 6:27; Romans 12:17–21

Biblical Illustrations—Hannah (1 Samuel 1); Jesus (1 Peter 2:21–23)

Work Ethic/Employment

See also Career, Laziness, Time Management

1. **God's plan for work was established from the very beginning—shortly after the creation of the world—and is therefore good.**

    Genesis 2:15 The LORD God took the man and put him in the Garden of Eden to work it and take care of it.

2. **Hard work continued in God's plan after sin entered the world.**

    Genesis 3:17–19 Cursed is the ground because of you; through painful toil you will eat of it all the days of your life. It will produce thorns and thistles for you, and you will eat the plants of the field. By the sweat of your brow you will eat your food until you return to the ground, since from it you were taken; for dust you are and to dust you will return.

3. **Working for our needs with our own hands is God's will.**

    1 Thessalonians 4:11–12 Make it your ambition to lead a quiet life, to mind your own business and to work with your hands, just as we told you, so that your daily life may win the respect of outsiders and so that you will not be dependent on anybody.

    Proverbs 21:25–26 The sluggard's craving will be the death of him, because his hands refuse to work. All day long he craves for more, but the righteous give without sparing.

    Psalm 90:17

4. **All work must be done with God's glory (and reputation) in mind.**

    Colossians 3:23 Whatever you do, work at it with all your heart, as working for the Lord, not for men.

1 Corinthians 10:31 So whether you eat or drink or whatever you do, do it all for the glory of God.

Ecclesiastes 12:13–14 Now all has been heard; here is the conclusion of the matter: Fear God and keep his commandments, for this is the whole duty of man. For God will bring every deed into judgment, including every hidden thing, whether it is good or evil.

Colossians 3:17

5. **Respectful obedience is due our employer. (For today's cultural application, substitute "workers" for "slaves" and "employers" for "masters.")**

Ephesians 6:5–8 Slaves, obey your earthly masters with respect and fear, and with sincerity of heart, just as you would obey Christ. Obey them not only to win their favor when their eye is on you, but like slaves of Christ, doing the will of God from your heart. Serve wholeheartedly, as if you were serving the Lord, not men, because you know that the Lord will reward everyone for whatever good he does, whether he is slave or free.

Titus 2:9–10 Teach slaves to be subject to their masters in everything, to try to please them, not to talk back to them, and not to steal from them, but to show that they can be fully trusted, so that in every way they will make the teaching about God our Savior attractive.

1 Timothy 6:1–2; 1 Peter 2:18–19

6. **We should enjoy work because God created us for it and gives us satisfaction in it.**

Ecclesiastes 5:18–19 Then I realized that it is good and proper for a man to eat and drink, and to find satisfaction in his toilsome labor under the sun during the few days of life God has given him—for this is his lot. Moreover, when God gives any man wealth and possessions, and enables him to enjoy them, to accept his lot and be happy in his work—this is a gift of God.

Ecclesiastes 3:12–13 I know that there is nothing better for men than to be happy and do good while they live. That everyone may eat and drink, and find satisfaction in all his toil—this is the gift of God.

7. **Note the example of the apostle Paul.**

1 Corinthians 4:12 We work hard with our own hands. When we are cursed, we bless; when we are persecuted, we endure it.

Acts 18:3 And because he was a tentmaker as they were, he stayed and worked with them.

1 Thessalonians 2:9 Surely you remember, brothers, our toil and hardship; we worked night and day in order not to be a burden to anyone while we preached the gospel of God to you.

Biblical Illustration—Joseph, in spite of his difficult situation (Genesis 39:2–5)

Worry

See also Depression, Fear, Trust

1. **The results of worry are negative and provide no help for the situation.**

   Proverbs 12:25 An anxious heart weighs a man down, but a kind word cheers him up.

   Job 6:1–3 Then Job replied: "If only my anguish could be weighed and all my misery be placed on the scales! It would surely outweigh the sand of the seas—no wonder my words have been impetuous."

   Matthew 6:27 Who of you by worrying can add a single hour to his life?

2. **Instead of worry, consider the proper response.**

   1 Peter 5:7 Cast all your anxiety on him because he cares for you.

   Philippians 4:6–7 Do not be anxious about anything, but in everything, by prayer and petition, with thanksgiving, present your requests to God. And the peace of God, which transcends all understanding, will guard your hearts and your minds in Christ Jesus.

   Isaiah 41:10, 13

3. **Anxiety is often fear of what *might be* rather than what *is*. Concentrate on what is true and positive.**

   Philippians 4:8 Finally, brothers, whatever is true, whatever is noble, whatever is right, whatever is pure, whatever is lovely, whatever is admirable—if anything is excellent or praiseworthy—think about such things.

   2 Timothy 1:7 For God did not give us a spirit of timidity, but a spirit of power, of love and of self-discipline.

4. God's sufficient resources are adequate for our every concern.

Philippians 4:13 I can do everything through him who gives me strength.

Philippians 4:19 And my God will meet all your needs according to his glorious riches in Christ Jesus.

2 Corinthians 12:9–10

5. Do we believe God is sovereign? The days God has given us are planned for our best interests. Trust puts anxiety to rest.

Psalm 139:16 Your eyes saw my unformed body. All the days ordained for me were written in your book before one of them came to be.

Isaiah 44:6 This is what the Lord says—Israel's King and Redeemer, the Lord Almighty: I am the first and I am the last; apart from me there is no God.

Isaiah 45:5–7

6. God can use anything for his ultimate plan. God wastes nothing.

Romans 8:28 And we know that in all things God works for the good of those who love him, who have been called according to his purpose.

7. Anxiety about the future is sheltered in God's ultimate plan.

Isaiah 26:3–4 You will keep in perfect peace him whose mind is steadfast, because he trusts in you. Trust in the Lord forever, for the Lord, the Lord, is the Rock eternal.

Matthew 6:33–34 But seek first his kingdom and his righteousness, and all these things will be given to you as well. Therefore do not worry about tomorrow, for tomorrow will worry about itself. Each day has enough trouble of its own.

John 14:1–3; 2 Thessalonians 3:16

Biblical Illustrations—Hannah (1 Samuel 1); Gideon (Judges 6)

Quick Scripture Reference
tools at your fingertips

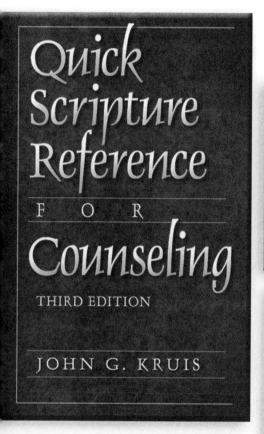

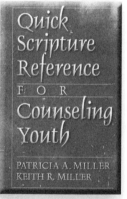

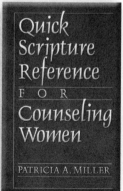

BakerBooks
Relevant. Intelligent. Engaging. a division of Baker Publishing Group www.bakerbooks.com